INTRODUCTION

IMAGINE IT IS 1962—just over fifty years ago. You are an African-American pastor living in Atlanta, Georgia, planning to visit the capital of your nation. Suppose this visit will be your first and, while you know many people who live in Washington, D.C., you've never been there yourself. This visit is important because this is a time of racial ferment in America, and you have something important to share with the Christians living in there.

So you write a letter to the Christians in Washington—black and white, man and woman, sympathetic and hostile—to introduce yourself and your ministry. More, since you plan for this letter to be read in public, you want to give a good account of what you believe and what you intend. Most of all, you want to persuade the readers of your love and your hopes—of God's love and hopes for them.

That, my friends, is exactly the challenge faced by the apostle Paul in approximately AD 56 when he wrote to the Christians in Rome. To raise the stakes of his letter,

Christians were then a minority and starting to suffer persecution by their neighbors and their government.

Paul knew how the Roman Christians suffered from the Edict of Claudius in AD 49, which evicted all Jews, including those believing in Jesus, from the city of Rome. When the decree was repealed after Claudius' death in AD 54, returning Jewish Christians found fellow believers among the Gentile population. During the absence of the Jewish believers, the Gentile believers in Rome had of necessity assumed leadership of the church. The two groups may have found each other's beliefs and practices strange, perhaps even blasphemous.

Paul very likely wrote to readers hostile to him and each other.

His letter to the Roman Christians departed from Paul's usual practice of writing only to communities or individuals to whom he had personally ministered—usually believers whom he had personally evangelized. The Roman believers he addressed, having picked up their faith second hand or perhaps in Jerusalem, might have followed varying, even conflicting versions of the gospel of Jesus Christ. Paul's message addressed that heterodoxy. Also the Holy Spirit may have moved him to write at this time to prepare for Paul's eventual ministry and martyrdom in Rome. This was a really important message, and Paul knew it. We should believe that he prayerfully did his best.

Modern Christians may forget that Paul wrote to Jewish and Gentile believers in Rome before most of the New Testament as we know it was written. In fact, the letters of Paul were among the first New Testament writings. So, he couldn't refer to the gospels, Acts of the Apostles, Hebrews or other epistles. His writing meshes so seamlessly with later, independent writings due to the guiding influence of the Holy Spirit.

In Romans, Paul built his message on the Lord Jesus Christ as revealed in the existing Jewish scriptures. Trained as a Pharisee, Paul knew what we call the Old Testament inside and out. In fact, his Letter to the Romans may be the most Old Testament dense book in the New Testament.

Paul also knew what he had preached and written previously. He had attended the first church Council in Jerusalem, which decided that most Old Testament practices and rituals did not apply to Gentile converts to Christianity. And he had lived as an evangelist for a dozen years—praying, proclaiming and defending the good news, often literally in the marketplaces of the Roman world. Each time I quote a New Testament source supporting Paul's argument, remember that the Holy Spirit hadn't inspired the writers of those gospels or epistles yet, making other New Testament agreement with the letter to the Romans that much more weighty— even supernatural.

That the circumstances of this writing are unique was underscored by his closing list of supporters many of whom might have been known to the Romans and therefore confirmed Paul's genuineness.

Because Paul employed a diatribe writing style—reproducing the give and take of an open discussion—his writing doesn't have the logical flow modern readers expect. Many readers tend to pick succinct quotes from Paul's letters but avoid them overall because his style seems so dense. Nevertheless a close and thoughtful study of this text reveals much good news for modern readers.

More important than its historical setting, Romans proves itself relevant to all Christians at all times. It is as though Paul and the Holy Spirit wrote it personally to you. Therefore, this study looks at Romans as a living document, relevant to our lives today. It progresses from theme to theme rather than strictly verse by verse. *Living in the Spirit* attempts to open the riches of Paul's message to modern readers.

This book is called *Living in the Spirit* drawing from both Paul's text and J. N. Darby's translation of Hebrews 11:1, that "Faith is the substantiating of things hoped for," not the substance or a similar noun found in many translations. The point is that our walking in faith (continually) brings into being in our lives what God has already accomplished on our behalf.

For that reason also much of this book is written in the present tense to capture the feeling of the Greek: action started in the past but continuing through the present into the future. This message of faith and our walking in it must be current and continuous to be real in our lives.

My principal sources are Paul's Letter to the Romans and other Biblical books as well as later Christian resources including Hans-Werner Bartsch's "The Historical Situation of Romans," Martin Luther's preface to Romans, Rick Joyner's *There Were Two Trees in the Garden*, A. W. Tozer's *Life in the Spirit* and *Man: The Dwelling Place of God*, Corrie ten Boom's *The Hiding Place*, Andrew Murray's *Abide in Christ*, and especially Watchman Nee's books *The Normal Christian Life*, *Release of the Spirit*, and *Sit, Walk and Stand*. The serious student will want to read all these books.

Paul outlined the basics of Christian transformation and life. In his letter he proclaimed the Christian basis for salvation: "a righteousness from God is revealed" that is available to everyone—Greek or Jew, man or woman, slave or free. He quoted Habakkuk 2:4, "the righteous will live by faith." From first to last Romans is about righteousness. Not the external righteousness of the worldly—even worldly Christians—but an inner transformation reflected in outward behavior. A righteousness from God.

Paul wrote to the Romans seeking a relationship with them which would "impart to you some spiritual gift to make you strong" (Romans 1:11). God has worked through Paul to save Christians across the ages and the world. God saved, is saving, will save you.

Join me in seeing what God may be saying to you through the pages of Paul's Letter to the Romans.

Before reading this book, I suggest you read Romans through. Just the text; not the notes or footnotes. Keep your Bible handy, so you can re-read the pertinent portions in context. Context is important. I have quoted the Bible and other sources liberally and at length that you may understand the context, but in some cases you'll want to read more.

Living in the Spirit exhorts you to a closer relationship with God. If these ideas don't work for you, seek others. Truth is not found in books but in Jesus Christ.

A few study questions follow each chapter suitable for individual or group study. Think about them. Write your answers down and look at them again later. Is that what you really think? Is that what you want to think?

One last clarification: Romans was written to Christians. Paul's opening negativism was not directed at the lost, but to those who thought they were saved. Jesus' whole ministry was about bringing mankind back into relationship with God. He loved the sinner, but likewise he was very short with the religious professionals of his day. And in Matthew 7:22-23 (NASB) Jesus warns that they will cry, "'Lord, Lord, did we not prophesy in Your name, and in Your name cast out demons, and in Your name perform many miracles?' And then I will declare to them, 'I never knew you; depart from me, you who practice lawlessness.'" We don't want to be among those shocked people.

This book is written to help you know God better and live a fuller life in his Spirit.

CHAPTER 1

Called to Jesus

Romans 1:1-17

◆

Paul opens his letter by introducing himself to the Christians in Rome. "Paul, a servant of Christ Jesus, called to be an apostle and set apart for the gospel of God" (Romans 1:1). The Roman Christians know him only by reputation, if at all. Both his calling and his separation underscore his qualifications to boldly address his readers.

As conveyed in Acts 9:3-6, the Lord Jesus Christ called Paul directly:

> As he was traveling, it happened that he was approaching Damascus, and suddenly a light from heaven flashed around him; and he fell to the ground and heard a voice saying to him, "Saul, Saul, why are

> you persecuting Me?" And he said, "Who are You, Lord?" And He said, "I am Jesus whom you are persecuting, but get up and enter the city, and it will be told you what you must do. (NASB)

Immediately afterward, the Lord sent Ananias to tell Saul that he was "his chosen instrument to carry my name before the Gentiles and their kings and before the people of Israel" (Acts 9:15).

Before his conversion Saul was a Pharisee, which means one who is separated. As Paul, he felt himself separated to preach the gospel to those who had not yet heard it, specifically to the Gentiles. "It has always been my ambition to preach the gospel where Christ was not known, so that I would not be building on someone else's foundation." (Romans 15:20)

The good news Paul proclaims is still available to and needed by all people. Many who already claim Jesus Christ as Lord don't know him or all that he did for them any more than those who haven't heard or who have rejected the gospel. Paul argues that God supernaturally provides for us—for all fallen humans through Jesus' sacrificial death and resurrection and the continuing presence of the Holy Spirit.

Because he doesn't know the people in Rome personally and they may not know him, Paul starts by detailing his relationship to Jesus and his office in the church. He especially reaches out to those of Jewish heritage by connecting the good news of Jesus Christ with the historical scriptures of the Jewish faith.

In fact, Paul doesn't even make it through his introduction before he introduces the core of his message of Jesus' lordship—and Paul's ministry—based on Christ's death and resurrection:

> The gospel [God] promised beforehand through his prophets in the Holy Scriptures regarding his Son, who as to his earthly life was a descendant of David, and who through the Spirit of holiness was appointed the Son of God in power by his resurrection from the dead: Jesus Christ our Lord. ... And you also are among those Gentiles who are called to belong to Jesus Christ. (Romans 1:2-4, 6)

Paul declares his goal of coming to Rome encourage and enlarge the group of believers there. He proclaims (Romans 1:17) the good news of Ezekiel 18:9 and Habakkuk 2:4 that "the righteous will live by faith." He then reminds his readers that the entire world needs this good news of salvation.

Okay, the righteous will live by faith, but what is faith? We'll explore a positive definition of faith—the one the Holy Spirit gave us—later, but for now let's establish what faith isn't.

Faith isn't something we do. It's not a work; it's a state of being—an active state of being.

- We "put our faith in Christ Jesus that we may be justified by faith in Christ and not by the works of the law, because by the works of the law no one will be justified" (Galatians 2:16).
- "For it is by grace you have been saved, through faith—and this is not from yourselves, it is the gift of God." (Ephesians 2:8)
- Jesus says, "Very truly I tell you, whoever hears my word and believes him who sent me has eternal life and will not be judged but has crossed over from death to life" (John 5:24).

Martin Luther reminds us that faith is more than believing. In fact, many moderns, both Christians and atheists, confuse believing God exists with having faith in God. Rick Joyner warns, "The delusion that mere intellectual agreement with certain biblical and historical facts is true faith has caused many to feel safe in a spiritual condition in which their spiritual lives may still be in jeopardy." While science disbelieves whatever cannot be quantified and measured, God invites us to test him.

- "Test me in this" (Malachi 3:10).
- "Taste and see that the LORD is good" (Psalm 34:8).
- "Whoever is kind to the poor lends to the LORD, and he will reward them for what they have done" (Proverbs 19:17).

- "And Jesus said, 'Give, and it will be given to you. A good measure, pressed down, shaken together and running over, will be poured into your lap. For with the measure you use, it will be measured to you'" (Luke 6:38).
- "In him and through faith in him we may approach God with freedom and confidence" (Ephesians 3:12).
- "Such confidence we have through Christ before God" (2 Corinthians 3:4).

Faith comes from believing deeply, truly and experientially.

Mere intellectual ascent to the Bible's validity or even Jesus' life and death doesn't save you; you're saved by your faith in Jesus.

> Having been buried with him in baptism, in which you were also raised with him through your faith in the working of God, who raised him from the dead. When you were dead in your sins and in the uncircumcision of your flesh, God made you alive with Christ. (Colossians 2:12-13)

God did the work. In advance. Before you sinned; before you were even born. We don't come to God by our faith as if building some emotional muscle. No, we accept that he's already done what is needed and allow him to plant the seed of faith in us.

That's not the end of it; it's barely the beginning. Faith isn't just believing with your mind, like setting a hat on your head. It's trusting with your life, like strapping on a parachute.

As Andrew Murray said, "Faith is ceasing all nature's efforts, and all other dependence; faith is confessed helplessness casting itself on God's promise, and claiming its fulfillment; faith is the putting ourselves quietly into God's hands for Him to do His work."

The good news is that not only may we know God by faith or do good works, but God wants a relationship with us. To achieve that closeness we must get beyond knowing that he exists, beyond knowing his rules well enough to teach them to others, beyond external manifestations of discipleship.

The world judges by externals: how tall, pretty, fast, or strong you were went a long way to establishing your credentials in ancient Rome, as it does in modern America. We may decry such superficiality, but even when we delve deeper, we often only look at accomplishments. We judge a person based on how his soul—his intellect, emotions, and will-power—manages his body. Even as Christians, we're deemed accomplished if we're smart, good, and self-controlled. But we may be all those things and still be totally separate from God.

Why don't we just elevate ourselves as people? Can't we think or feel or will ourselves into God's presence? No. In fact, those who try are just the people Paul addresses. He first warns the man who seeks God in nature, second the man who is self-controlled to the point of judging others, and finally the man who takes it upon himself to instruct others.

God isn't content with us knowing who he is; he wants us to know him and love him as he has known and loved us since before the universe was created. He makes clear from the first that the good news (gospel) of salvation is for everyone—whether Jew or Greek.

The Jewish and Greek division wasn't just a racial or religious classification. In Paul's day, and especially from the Jewish point of view, all humans were either the chosen people or they weren't. Those not included in the people—the Jews—were the nations (*Goyim*). (We'll discuss the implications of that dichotomy in chapter 11.)

Likewise, the Greeks tended to divide everyone into Greeks and barbarians. We haven't changed much in twenty centuries. We still divide "us" and "them"— everybody else.

But Paul wants both Jews and Gentiles to know that the good news is for all—no exclusions. "For in the gospel the righteousness of God is revealed—a righteousness that is by faith from first to last, just as it is written: 'The righteous will live by faith'" (Romans 1:17, quoting Habakkuk 2:4).

Of course, many of Paul's contemporaries, like many of ours, didn't think they needed saving. They may have looked around and judged themselves to be better than other people, and certainly no worse. So first Paul has to address the human condition—their condition and ours.

What he found wasn't and isn't pretty.

Study Questions

Chapter 1
Called to Jesus

1. Paul, a Jewish Pharisee and a Roman citizen, identifies himself as a servant of Jesus Christ. What credential is most important to you? How does our self-image affect our message? Why is knowing who you are and what you live for important?

2. Before completing his introduction, Paul presents the good news of Jesus Christ our Lord. How would you open a letter to a group of Christians you've never met?

3. Why is faith important?

4. Is your relationship with God based on belief or faith. What difference does it make?

CHAPTER 2

Under Wrath

Romans 1:18 - 3:20

◆

Paul plunges into declaring not the good news but the bad: God isn't happy.

"The wrath of God is being revealed from heaven against all the godlessness and wickedness of men who suppress the truth by their wickedness" (Romans 1:18). God is angry because pretty much everyone believes their own imaginings and not God's truth. In Romans 1 and 2, Paul lists three categories of law breakers to whom the rest of his message is addressed. Not surprisingly, his list includes many who call themselves Christians but in increasingly tighter focus.

First, Paul faults those who "suppress the truth by their wickedness" (Romans 1:18). Modern readers, since Paul spent a few verses addressing the rampant homosexuality in the Roman world (as well as ours), may think the sin Paul talked about is homosexuality. It's not. Paul declares, "Men are without excuse" for not knowing "what may be known about God ... his eternal power and divine nature" (Romans 1:19-20).

Permit me the first of many digressions. In verse 20, Paul is not arguing for a natural theology, one that abstracts God's existence from his acts. Instead, he declares that the revealed triune God could be clearly seen acting in nature.

God's existence is declared, not argued.

- "In the beginning God ..." (Genesis 1:1).
- "In the beginning was the Word, and the Word was with God, and the Word was God" (John 1:1).
- "Very truly I tell you," Jesus answered, "before Abraham was born, I am!" (John 8:58).
- "And now, Father, glorify me in your presence with the glory I had with you before the world began" (John 17:5).
- "Do you not know? Have you not heard? Has it not been told you from the beginning? Have you not understood since the earth was founded? He sits enthroned above the circle of the earth, and its people are like grasshoppers. He stretches out the heavens like a canopy, and spreads them out like a tent to live in" (Isaiah 40:21-22 and Acts 17:24 NASB).

In the Bible God is a fact, not a conclusion.

Whatever you may think of non-scriptural proofs of God's existence, we need no proof that we, like the Romans and Corinthians of Paul's day, go our merry way inventing new paths of evil. Look at the evening news.

The point is not whether those arguments are logically sufficient; the point is that "what may be known about God … his eternal power and divine nature—have been clearly seen, being understood from what has been made, so that men are without excuse" (Romans 1:19-20).

These men neither glorify God nor thank him. They claim to be wise but abandon "the glory of the immortal God for images made to look like mortal man and birds and animals and reptiles" (Romans 1:23).

Idolatry.

That's the sin Paul decries. Making idols of created things while denying the very existence of the one who created them and us. You smirk and say to yourself, "Well, at least I'm not that stupid." No?

Pause and consider the infamy of the Jews in the Wilderness. These very people had seen the sea part for them to pass to safety and close to destroy the Egyptian army. They were miraculously watered and fed in the desert. And as soon as Moses goes out of their sight to worship God, they say, "Come, make us gods who will go before us. As for this fellow Moses who brought us up out of Egypt, we don't know what has happened to him" (Exodus 32:1).

"This fellow Moses?" As if he was some stranger to them. As if they needed a god they could see. So Aaron casts the image of a calf from gold and says, "These are your gods, O Israel, who brought you out of Egypt" (Exodus 32:4). What a kick in God's teeth.

We moderns may have gotten beyond calves cast of gold, but not as far as we'd like to think. Don't we still worship gold—or maybe the almighty dollar? Don't we make idols of things we created: houses, cars, jewelry, clothes, electronic devices? Don't we idolize movie stars, singers, athletes, politicians and pastors?

Even worse, many who call ourselves Christians worship a Jesus shaped by ourselves. Many churches today obey the word of God only to the extent it doesn't interfere with our pleasure. End the service before the kickoff. Don't offend anyone. Divorce, abortion, homosexuality— not to mention lying, greed, and pride—are all okay with many modern Christians.

Our stubbornness is idolatry because we put ourselves on the throne of God. The shape of the idol may have changed, but the sin of idolatry remains.

"Because of this," Paul says, "God gave them over to shameful lusts" (Romans 1:26). God was not the source of those lusts; he just allows us to reap what we have sowed.

This is about far more and far worse than homosexuality, as Paul's laundry list of sins illustrates:

> Filled with every kind of wickedness, evil,
> greed and depravity. They are full of envy,

> murder, strife, deceit and malice. They are
> gossips, slanderers, God-haters, insolent,
> arrogant and boastful; they invent ways of
> doing evil; they disobey their parents; they
> have no understanding, no fidelity, no love,
> no mercy. (Romans 1:29-31)

Why? Because "Just as they did not see fit to acknowledge God any longer, God gave them over to a depraved mind, to do those things which are not proper" (Romans 1:28 NASB).

So, our first sin is idolatry. And what is God's judgment? "Although they know God's righteous decree that those who do such things deserve death, they not only continue to do these very things but also approve of those who practice them" (Romans 1:32).

Which brings us to Paul's second category of sin: hypocrisy.

"You, therefore, have no excuse, you who pass judgment on someone else, for at whatever point you judge another, you are condemning yourself, because you who pass judgment do the same things" (Romans 2:1).

Jesus asked, "Why do you look at the speck of sawdust in your brother's eye and pay no attention to the plank in your own eye?" (Luke 6:4). Like those hypocrites, we pass judgment on others for the very things we do ourselves, and thereby "show contempt for the riches of his kindness, tolerance and patience" (Romans 2:4).

Men are as universally guilty of this condemnation as the first one.

Over and over Jesus warns us, "Do not judge, or you too will be judged" (Matthew 7:1). "Let any one of you who is without sin be the first to throw a stone at her" (John 8:7). And, returning to Romans, "So when you, a mere human being, pass judgment on them and yet do the same things, do you think you will escape God's judgment?" (Romans 2:3).

Here Paul introduces another of Romans major themes: the law. Rather than being saved by the law, as the Jews supposed, Paul points out,

> For it is not the hearers of the Law who are just before God, but the doers of the Law will be justified. For when Gentiles who do not have the Law do instinctively the things of the Law, these, not having the Law, are a law to themselves, in that they show the work of the Law written in their hearts, their conscience bearing witness and their thoughts alternately accusing or else defending them, on the day when, according to my gospel, God will judge the secrets of men through Christ Jesus (Romans 2:13-16 NASB).

Our outward declarations or actions don't save or condemn us so much as our inner secrets. This is why Peter warns against false teachers also. "If they have escaped the corruption of the world by knowing our Lord and Savior Jesus Christ and are again entangled in it and are overcome, they are worse off at the end than they were at the beginning" (2 Peter 2:20).

We Christians can be so puffed up in our own eyes that we instruct others at the very points of our disobedience. We are false teachers. Make no mistake, our pride-borne deception is equally as bad as our idolatry and hypocrisy. Our Lord said,

> "It is inevitable that stumbling blocks come,
> but woe to him through whom they come!
> It would be better for him if a millstone
> were hung around his neck and he were
> thrown into the sea, than that he would
> cause one of these little ones to stumble."
> (Luke 17:1-2)

So the second category of sin is hypocrisy and brings us to the third: pride.

Paul addresses the Jews first. "You call yourself a Jew; if you rely on the law and boast in God" (Romans 2:17).

Then he runs through a laundry list of things about which they may be proud.

> If you know his will and approve of what
> is superior because instructed in the law, if
> you are convinced that you are a guide for
> the blind, a light for those who are in the
> dark, an instructor of the foolish, a teacher

> of little children, because you have in the law the embodiment of knowledge and truth. (Romans 2:18-19)

With all these advantages, he asks, why then do you break the very laws you teach?

Paul fingers those who brag about their special status under the law, Jews or Christians, yet broke those laws themselves. "God does not show favoritism," Paul declares (Romans 2:11). We think ourselves superior, being "confident that you yourself are a guide to the blind, a light to those who are in darkness, a corrector of the foolish, a teacher of the immature ..." (Romans 2:19-20 NASB). He asks rhetorically, "You who brag about the law, do you dishonor God by breaking the law?" (Romans 2:23).

Therefore, he quotes Isaiah 52:5, "God's name is blasphemed among the Gentiles because of you" (Romans 2:24). Yes, because of us.

We, like the Jews of Paul's day, are supposed to be the light of the world, the city on a hill. And God is dishonored because of us. No wonder Paul is down on them. We fall under the same judgment. We're in trouble, people. Paul described how religion has become a stumbling block to his fellow Jews, concluding that "no one is righteous" (Romans 3:10).

You get a better feeling for Paul's indictment of the Jews if you read the first half of Romans 3, substituting the words "Christian" for "Jew" and "baptism" for "circumcision." Are you shocked and offended? How do you think Paul's Jewish readers felt? Sometimes, as Gloria Garner says, "God will offend your mind, so He can get to your heart."

Paul ends his indictments with,

> Now we know that whatever the Law says, it speaks to those who are under the Law, so that every mouth may be closed and all the world may become accountable to God; because by the works of the Law no flesh will be justified in His sight; for through the Law comes the knowledge of sin. (Romans 3:19-20 NASB)

Are you conscious of your sin? Are you condemned by your own lifestyle or thought life? Do you judge others, but give yourself a pass? Do you proudly forward Christian emails to all the Christians on your mailing list but continue to contemplate, if not indulge, in that sin that only you (and God) knows about?

This is the bad news with which Paul opens his letter to the Christians in Rome. The sins he identified—idolatry, false teaching and religious pride—are as relevant today as then. Make no mistake: Paul wrote this letter to Christians. Not unconverted Jews. Not pagans. They and we are guilty of those same sins.

In our day many people are named on the church rolls, attend once a week, and give something when the plate goes by—if they give substantially, they demand a brass plaque proclaiming their generosity. A. W. Tozer calls these people "social Christians." Or you could call them nominal Christians—Christians in name only. Many of them are going to hell. No, I'm not judging them; they have judged themselves.

> When we see sin in all its hideousness and enormity, the Holiness of God in all its perfection, and the glory of Jesus Christ in all its infinity, nothing but a doctrine that those who persist in … the rejection of the Son of God, shall endure everlasting anguish, will satisfy the demands of our own moral institutions.
>
> — R. A. Torrey

Many of us are or were just like those social Christians. We are lost; we are carnal; we are orphans; we are condemned. In our natural state—Paul would say, in our "religious" state—we are doomed.

To illustrate Paul's theme, think of an automobile gas gauge as a metaphor for how full our spiritual "tank" is. Our tanks start empty. Not only is the needle somewhere below "E" but the warning light is on, and the warning bell is ringing. We can't even start our engines, let alone go anywhere.

However, unlike whoever sold you your car, God prepared a way to fill your tank and keep it full. First, of course, we have to call for his roadside assistance.

Study Questions

Chapter 2
Under Wrath

1. Paul identifies three areas where supposed believers demonstrate their godlessness. Are they valid today? How would you get the attention of your readers?
2. Why do you think modern people find the idea of judgment repugnant?
3. Complacency threatens those who think they are safe. Identify three ways you are complacent and identify how to counteract that in yourself as well as your friends and family.
4. Are you trusting some religious rite—recent or past—to put you right with God? How might that be perilous?
5. Charles Spurgeon wrote, "It is the work of the Spirit of God to convince men of sin, and until they are convinced of sin, they will never be led to seek the righteousness that God gives by Jesus Christ." What strengthens or weakens your sense of sin?
6. Why do people resist the idea that they need God's salvation?

CHAPTER 3

FORGIVENESS

Romans 3:21 - 24

◆

PAUL DIDN'T BELABOR how lost and hopeless the Romans (and we) were before Jesus saved us. You already know that. In fact, if Christians have done anything well these last centuries it's pointing out the depravity and need of the world. So, Paul presses immediately into revealing God's provision for our doomed condition.

How are we to be saved from our lives of sin? Paul begins his great exposition of the basis for our hope with the following words:

> But now apart from the Law the righteousness of God has been manifested, being witnessed by the Law and the Prophets, even the righteousness of God through faith in Jesus Christ for all those

> who believe; for there is no distinction; for
> all have sinned and fall short of the glory of
> God, being justified as a gift by His grace
> through the redemption which is in Christ
> Jesus. (Romans 3:21-24 NASB)

Do you get it? God so loves the world. (see John 3:16) He so loves you—each of you—that he provided everything we need to be fully restored. Not just saved. Not just sanctified, but remade into the children he designed us to be—who he designed Adam and Eve to be. And he did it all long before you were born. Long before you sinned. Long before you were lost. Why? Because, like the sheep which had gone astray in Jesus' parable, "your Father in heaven is not willing that any of these little ones should be lost" (Matthew 18:14).

God's answer to all the issues of life is his son, our Lord Jesus Christ. As Paul tells the Galatians, the end result is that, "I no longer live, but Christ lives in me" (2:20). That's it. Everything else is footnotes. Jesus' blood, Jesus' death, Jesus' burial, Jesus' resurrection, Jesus' ascension, Jesus' spirit. It's all about Jesus, and nothing about me. "For God so loved the world that he gave his one and only Son, that whoever believes in him shall not perish but have eternal life" (John 3:16).

Love? Didn't Paul just declare how angry God is with us? He did. God is angry with us—both Jews and Christians—because we are just like the Pharisees Jesus castigated for their hypocrisy and bad example. But how did Jesus act toward the tax collectors, the woman taken in adultery, and the children? He showed them, who knew no better, love. And we supposedly have received that love since we claim his name.

"If I claim the name of Christ, he claims my body as his temple," Sy Rogers tells us. Many of us have trouble turning control of our bodies to God, but be assured he wants much more than just our bodies. He wants all of us, that we might receive all of him.

He loves each of us as much as he loved Adam or Eve. Before he created them he knew they would sin, just as he knew we would sin. So, he made provision—in advance—to forgive us our sins, to free us from bondage to sin, and for us to fulfill the purpose he designed for all mankind. And he did it before he put the first star in the sky.

Paul spends the next five chapters of Romans detailing how the righteousness of God is offered to us; and how, if we don't appropriate all God offers, we may not be operating in the fullness—in the power of his grace. In fact, many of us, though we are saved from sin, are not saved from the law of sin nor have we surrendered the mastery of our lives to the Holy Spirit.

We are not living in the Spirit.

Thus, while we are profoundly better off than we were before we were saved, we fall far short of the glory for which God designed us. And God so loves us that he's not content that we should live outside of that fullness. That peace. That love.

To fully understand and operate in God's grace, we must know what we were saved from and what the mechanism of our salvation was.

But let me hasten to declare two things:

First, this understanding is not the basis for your salvation; your faith in Jesus is that foundation. But something subtle is going on here—something perhaps diabolical—which does affect our freedom to operate in all that God has made available to us. Something that tries to keep us ignorant of and not operating in all he has done, and is doing, and will do for us. Paul's letter to the Romans and this book seek to identify and rectify that unconsciousness.

Second, while Paul's writing picks apart the mechanism of our salvation, neither he nor I intend that you should believe that the blood, the cross, the grave, the resurrection, baptism, communion or any other detail of God's plan works in a vacuum. It's just that the gift of God is so rich and so full that we might be tempted to gloss over the details and therefore miss the fullness of God's grace. Such may have been the state of the Roman Christians two thousand years ago, and certainly is the state of many American Christians today.

God plans much more for us than we have so far appropriated. "Immeasurably more than all we ask or imagine, according to his power that is at work within us" (Ephesians 3:20). It's as if he prepared a huge banquet for us, but we insist on staying in the anteroom eating the hors d'oeuvres. No, my friends, what most of us have experienced so far in our Christian life is merely the snack before the meal. The pre-game show before the Super Bowl. The short cartoon before the featured film.

God's provision is a package deal. Even though the Holy Spirit led Paul into this detailed exposition, we get it all, if we will just appropriate it. All of it. Like one of those infomercials where the huckster keeps yelling, "But, wait, there's more." Because there is more, my friend, so very much more.

It's all Jesus, and it's all good.

Study Questions

Chapter 3
Forgiveness

1. How can Jesus be the sole and sufficient answer to our sins? To the evil of the world? Does this sound too good to be true?
2. What fullness do you think God offers? What is missing from your life? How might you remedy that deficiency?
3. Why it is impossible to stand perfect before God based on the law?

CHAPTER 4

His Blood is Sufficient

Romans 3: 22 - 30

---◆---

To FULLY UNDERSTAND what Paul means by God providing us a righteousness—before the law, before sin—through which we are restored to the status and relationship to God which Adam enjoyed before the fall, we must look again at the Old Testament. In fact, only through this provision of God are we empowered to be what Adam was designed to be, but never was due to his sin and separation from God. Think of it, we should aspire not to just what Adam was before he sinned, but what he would have been, but wasn't.

Picking up at Romans 3:22-25:

> This righteousness from God comes through faith in Jesus Christ to all who believe.

> There is no difference, for all have sinned and fall short of the glory of God, and are justified freely by his grace through the redemption that came by Christ Jesus. God presented him as a sacrifice of atonement, through faith in his blood.

In one paragraph Paul mentions four key concepts: justification by grace, redemption, atonement through Jesus' sacrifice, and faith in the blood. All to free us from the consequences of sin.

Sin enters our lives as disobedience. We remove ourselves from fellowship with God. Remember how God sought Adam and Eve in the garden, but they hid themselves? "Then the man and his wife heard the sound of the LORD God as he was walking in the garden in the cool of the day, and they hid from the LORD God among the trees of the garden" (Genesis 3: 8).

Why did they hide themselves? Because of guilt. "[Adam] answered, 'I heard you in the garden, and I was afraid because I was naked; so I hid.' And [God] said, 'Who told you that you were naked? Have you eaten from the tree that I commanded you not to eat from?'" (Genesis 3:10-11). Adam and Eve knew they had disobeyed; so they hid.

Sin first removes us from the presence of God, then guilt—our knowledge of our sin; our consciences accusing us—breaks our relationship with God. Finally, sin gives Satan ground to accuse us before God and in our hearts.

God knew this would happen. Therefore he provides a means to deal with all three: our sin, our guilt and Satan's accusation. The blood of Christ. Not surprisingly, it works in three ways: God-ward, man-ward and Satan-ward. (This model is from Watchman Nee's *Normal Christian Life*.) Jesus died as our substitute on the Cross. His blood is sufficient and effective to cleanse our sin, our guilt and finally to cancel the claims of Satan against us.

First, look at the Godward aspect. Jesus' blood is our atonement. He took our place on the cross. God forgives our sins not because he ignores them. Oh, no, we really sinned, and he really can't stand sin. It'd be better to say that he won't tolerate sin. Nothing we can do merits God's pardon. But our sins are forgiven because when he looks at our sins what he sees is the blood of Jesus. Jesus died to atone for our sin. (To live in that atonement, of course, we must repent of our sins and receive its benefits, as we'll discuss later.)

Simply and scripturally, Jesus died in our place. We've already established that we're all sinners, unfit for any mercy from our creator. As unrepentant sinners we're also unfit to even seek forgiveness. But that same creator set in motion the means of our justification, our sanctification and our glorification before we drew our first breath. The shed blood of Jesus accomplishes many things. To understand, let's review the role of blood in the Bible.

Starting in Genesis, nearly every holy moment of the Old Testament is sealed with blood. Why blood? Man had already determined that life was bound to the blood.

Men and animals survived many types of wounds, but died quickly when bled out of even a minor seeming cut.

God already knew that he planned to come down as the ultimate sacrifice. So he established blood as a specific symbol.

Blood is first mentioned in Genesis 4:10-11 (NASB), when the LORD said [to Cain], "What have you done? The voice of your brother's blood is crying to Me from the ground. Now you are cursed from the ground, which has opened its mouth to receive your brother's blood from your hand."

Immediately we see that blood had significance beyond its life-sustaining function. Blood is a symbol for life itself and for guilt and innocence.

To Noah, God said,

> Every moving thing that is alive shall be food for you; I give all to you, as I gave the green plant. Only you shall not eat flesh with its life, that is, its blood. Surely I will require your lifeblood; from every beast I will require it. And from every man, from every man's brother I will require the life of man. Whoever sheds man's blood, by man his blood shall be shed, for in the image of God he made man. (Genesis 9:3-6 NASB)

Blood and its shedding held a high place in the culture and worship of the Old Testament, long before the Law was given to Moses.

Circumcision was as much a blood ceremony as some early hygiene technique. God told Abram, "This is My covenant, which you shall keep, between Me and you and your descendants after you: every male among you shall be circumcised. Thus shall My covenant be in your flesh for an everlasting covenant" (Genesis 17:10, 13 NASB).

To Moses, God said, "For the life of a creature is in the blood, and I have given it to you to make atonement for yourselves on the altar; it is the blood that makes atonement for one's life" (Leviticus 17:11).

A hundred times in the Old and New Testaments, blood is connected with atonement, and note that it is always something for God, not for man.

In Leviticus 16, we find the rules for the Day of Atonement, where the blood of the sin offering is taken into the Holy of Holies and sprinkled before God seven times.

Look at the first Passover in Exodus 12. That Passover, and its annual commemoration which devout Jews celebrate to this day, is a prototype for the death of Jesus. Again in that case, the blood was for God, not for man. (Exodus 12:13) "… when I see the blood, I will pass over you." Do you see it?

So, the value of Jesus' blood is not what we estimate it to be, it's what God knows it to be: the Paschal Lamb— sinless, without spot or blemish. "Behold the Lamb of God who takes away the sin of the world" (John 1:29).

Second, the blood works manward. It deals with our consciousness of our sin: our guilt. Before we were saved, sin didn't bother us. Our consciences were asleep, unconscious, dead. We had consciences, but mostly they weren't functioning. We could rationalize anything. Sound familiar?

But once we were saved, our consciences woke up and began to not only warn us away from temptation, but also accuse us of unforgiven sin. For some of us, it actually became a stumbling block because all we could see was our sin and guilt. We began to think that our sins were bigger than Jesus' atonement.

The problem was that we were trying to figure this out for ourselves. We were trying to feel, as it were, the effectiveness of the blood. And we didn't. We can't. It doesn't work that way.

Remember: the blood is first of all for God. It's his estimation, not ours, of what it's worth that counts. How do we know how he values the blood? He told us.

> Knowing that you were not redeemed with perishable things like silver or gold from your futile way of life inherited from your forefathers, but with precious blood, as of a lamb unblemished and spotless, the blood of Christ. (1 Peter 1:18-19 NASB)

If God accepts the blood, we are assured the debt is paid.

Here's how it works: Our hearts are fatally sick. Jeremiah declared, "The heart is deceitful above all things and beyond cure" (Romans 17:9). Did you get that? "Beyond cure." Our heart (not our bodily heart, but our spiritual heart—the center of our being) can't just be cleansed, it must be crucified. (We'll talk about that shortly.)

For now it is enough to know that we can only be cured by a heart transplant. God arranged that too. Ezekiel 36:26 explains: "I will give you a new heart and put a new spirit in you; I will remove from you your heart of stone and give you a heart of flesh."

Before going on, we need to correct the idea that the blood just cleanses the heart; it doesn't. We're too far gone for that. Hebrews 12:22 speaks of "having our hearts sprinkled to cleanse us from a guilty conscience."

But notice what's happening is the cleansing of a guilty conscience—the very thing we were discussing—not the cleansing of our heart. The blood of Christ is the means, but the object is our guilt.

Something got between me and God—my sin—which resulted in me having a guilty conscience, which keeps reminding me of my separation from God. Like David, "For I know my transgressions, and my sin is ever before me" (Psalm 51:3 NASB). How can we pray or praise God with the filth of our sins ever in front of us? We can't.

What does the blood do? It removes the barrier. And our conscience is cleaned. Having a clear conscience is important because, when our conscience is accusing us, it drains our faith away; and we find that we have lost contact with God. He's still there but our sin—our guilt—blocks our seeing him. How dare we think we can contemplate entering the Holy of Holies—God's very presence—but by the blood of Jesus?

What then does "by the blood" mean? It means that I recognize my sins—yes, the one I committed just now (I hope I asked forgiveness yesterday for my sin yesterday). I recognize my current sin, and I confess my need for cleansing and atonement. I approach God based on the finished work of Jesus. Nothing I have ever done or can ever do merits his approval, let alone his presence.

Many of us think God has set some standard of behavior which *we* must meet, and only by meeting that standard can we enter his presence. I'll act a little better; I'll be a little more patient; I'll read the Bible a little more.

No! "You foolish Galatians!" (Galatians 3:1). Who told you that? Nothing we can do can clear our consciences; only the shed blood of Jesus. And if I don't read four chapters of the Bible every day, or don't come to church every time the door is open, or "amen" the loudest, does that mean I can't approach God? No, no, a thousand times, no.

Your basis for approaching God is not how you feel; it's Jesus' blood that was shed for you. God looks at you—dirty, sinful, failing again and again—and he sees the blood of Jesus.

You dare not trust in anything less. His blood is the same yesterday, today and tomorrow. His blood is always sufficient. His merit; not yours.

So, approach God boldly because you depend on the blood, not on anything of yourself. Go into the Holy of Holies and commune with your Lord. Whether you've had a bad day, or lost your temper, or worse yet if you think you've been good (because you know you haven't—not under your own power).

You can only approach him based on the shed blood of Jesus. Nothing else.

"But now in Christ Jesus you who formerly were far off have been brought near by the blood of Christ" (Ephesians 2:13 NASB). You worry, "Yes, I loved God and confessed and was saved, but I've sinned since then." So? Nothing has changed.

> Therefore, brothers and sisters, since we have confidence to enter the Most Holy Place by the blood of Jesus, . . . let us draw near to God with a sincere heart and with the full assurance that faith brings, having our hearts sprinkled to cleanse us from a guilty conscience and having our bodies washed with pure water. (Hebrews 10:19, 22 NASB)

You still have to bathe your natural body daily, don't you? Well, even more so you need to confess your sins and appropriate the blood of Jesus every day.

You think you've moved beyond the A, B, Cs of the good news? No, you haven't. Our first approach was based on the blood, our approach today is based on the blood, and so it will be until we join him in glory—also based on his blood.

We may be weak, but focusing on our weakness doesn't make us strong. No, we shouldn't just go on sinning and let God get more glory (as Paul rightly condemns in Romans 6:1), but we never outgrow our need for the precious blood of Jesus. "Blessed is the man whose sin the Lord will never count against him" (Romans 4:8).

Okay, we've dealt with the Godward and the manward value of the blood, let's look at our Accuser. In Revelation 12:10, John calls Satan, "the accuser of our brothers, who accuses them before our God day and night."

Since the fall, man has been literally and metaphorically outside the garden—out from under the spiritual covering of God. "For all have sinned and fall short of the glory of God," (Romans 3:23) and our guilt has separated ourselves from God.

Not just sin generalized, but each and every particular sin. Not that I know myself that well, or God doesn't. Or that I can hide it from God. No, his light exposes everything. "But if we walk in the Light as He Himself is in the light, we have fellowship with one another, and the blood of Jesus His Son cleanses us from all sin" (1 John 1:7 NASB).

The blood of Jesus is absolutely sufficient. "When Christ came as high priest … he entered the Most Holy Place once for all by his own blood, having obtained eternal redemption" (Hebrews 9:11-12). He redeemed us once, but he stands now (and forever) as our high priest and our advocate, and "He is the atoning sacrifice for our sins" (1 John 2:1-2).

If God, seeing our sins in the light of the blood, forgives us; on what grounds can Satan accuse us? Oh, he will accuse us. But "If God is for us, who is against us? Who will bring a charge against God's elect? God is the one who justifies" (Romans 8:31,33 NASB).

And Satan? He still accuses us, not only to God but to our consciences. He claims, "You're weak. You've sinned. You'll keep on sinning."

Make no mistake, it's true; but less so than you'd think, as we'll explore below. We fall into Satan's trap if we then try to defend ourselves through our own righteousness or our own works. Neither is sufficient, but likewise we should not just give up and yield to despair, let alone yielding to sin. Don't be fooled.

That accusation is Satan's most powerful weapon against you. Not because we haven't been cleansed, but because we act as if we haven't. We play into his hands if we accept the accusation and try to defend ourselves based on our own merits.

We can put no confidence in ourselves. Yes, we sinned. That's what flesh does. Sin is our nature, but it does not have to be our destiny. But if we side with the accuser, we deserve death.

Only God can answer this accusation. And he has. Already. By the shedding of his precious blood on our behalf.

Don't look to yourself; look to Jesus. As John the Baptist said, "Behold, the Lamb of God who takes away the sin of the world!" (John 1:29 NASB). We are sinful, but the blood of Jesus cleanses us from all sin.

Paul wrote, "Who will bring any charge against God's elect? God is the one who justifies; who is the one who condemns? Christ Jesus is He who died, yes, rather who was raised to life, who is at the right hand of God, who also intercedes for us" (Romans 8:33-34 NASB).

Jesus intervened for us on the cross; he still intercedes for us today.

Why are we trying to base our forgiveness on our own righteousness? Remember: "The blood of Jesus His Son cleanses us from all sin" (1 John 1:7). It's Jesus' blood that only, always saves us.

Satan will continue accusing us until Judgment Day. "For the accuser of our brothers and sisters, who accuses them before our God day and night . . ." (Revelation 12:10). But we must not listen to his argument. God doesn't.

"The blood of Christ … cleanse[s] our consciences" (Hebrews 9:14). So, Satan-ward, the blood cleanses our consciences, so that we need not shy away from God in guilt. God can and has dealt with our sins, but he can't save us if we don't trust in the blood to be all sufficient.

Oh, yes, there's much more. But right here, right now, know that if you haven't approached God on the basis of the shed blood of Jesus, you haven't approached him at all.

Nothing you can do suffices. That's why your prayers go unanswered; that's why you are crippled by guilt and unforgiveness; that's why you sin the same sin over and over despite your best intentions and efforts. That's why you aren't living in grace and power.

But the blood *is* there. It's been available to each of us since before we sinned—before we were born. Forgiveness is ready for you. Your sins are forgiven by what Jesus did two thousand years ago. Your life, your sin was exchanged for Jesus' sinless life. Nothing you did merits it. Nothing you can do makes you deserve it nor can you earn it. It's done.

All you must do is to receive it.

Where has Paul taken us so far? He established that we have no basis to claim we are anything but dirty, rotten sinners. And he started us down the road to redemption. The road that starts at the cross of Jesus and is liberally sprinkled with his shed blood. Justified. Our lives have been moved out of "bad" and into "good", if we are in Jesus.

In terms of our spiritual gas gauge, we're got enough in our tanks to move the needle off empty. We aren't full by any means—the low fuel warning may still be on—but we can at least start our engines.

As John Newton wrote, "We were lost, now we're found. Slave, but now we're free."

Study Questions

Chapter Four
His Blood is Sufficient

1. How do you know you are justified before God?
2. Do you believe that Jesus' blood atones for your sin, cleanses your guilty conscience, and deflects Satan's accusations? If not, why not?
3. Do you receive the finished work of Jesus?

CHAPTER 5

FAITH NOT WORKS

Romans 4:1 - 24

◆

MANY OF US are tempted to skip over Romans 4 as Paul argues how Abraham was justified by his faith, not his works. We think we know all that. Do we?

In fact, many of us—even Christians—live our lives as if we are earning our way into heaven. Others of us act like we're trying for a different destination. But we can't just skip by this discussion of faith; it is the key to opening our relationship with God.

First, we might ask, why Abraham? Why not one of the other faithful? Such as those listed in the litany of the faithful in Hebrews. Perhaps because Abraham was the last common father of both Jews and Gentiles. (In fact a significant number of his own descendants were excluded from the covenant nation, as we'll discuss in chapter 12.)

The book of Hebrews provides us a good working definition of faith: "Now faith is confidence in what we hope for and assurance about what we do not see" (Hebrews 1.1). Gerri Dickens reminds us, "You have to get out of yourself—beyond your situation. Then you can see God."

"Faith always has been the mark of God's servants, from the beginning of the world," Matthew Henry tells us. "Where the principle is planted by the regenerating Spirit of God, it will cause the truth to be received, concerning justification by the sufferings and merits of Christ." Faith unlocks the door to our hearts, allowing the Holy Spirit to enter.

Inevitably, you will ask, what about James? Didn't James say, "What good is it, my brothers and sisters, if someone claims to have faith but has no deeds? Can such faith save them?" (James 2:14). He did. But he also said, "You see that [Abraham's] faith and his actions were working together, and his faith was made complete by what he did."

How do we reconcile this apparent paradox?

Martin Luther resolved it five hundred years ago, but we need to re-learn the lesson. In his Preface to Romans, Luther wrote,

> [The Jews] have to inherit Abraham's faith
> if they want to be his real heirs, since it
> was prior to the Law of Moses and the law
> of circumcision that Abraham became just

through faith and was called a father of all believers. ... The law brings about more wrath than grace, because no one obeys it with love and eagerness.

Interestingly, both Paul and James quote Genesis 15:6 ("Abraham believed God, and it was credited to him as righteousness.") in their respective discussions of faith versus works. In a sense, they're both right. Paul is looking to motives; James to actions (See also Galatians 3:6-25).

Luther explains,

"Outwardly you keep the law with works out of fear of punishment or love of gain. Likewise you do everything without free desire and love of the law; you act out of aversion and force. You'd rather act otherwise if the law didn't exist. It follows, then, that you, in the depths of your heart, are an enemy of the law."

He also writes,

"To fulfill the law means to do its work eagerly, lovingly and freely, without the constraint of the law; it means to live well and in a manner pleasing to God, as though there were no law or punishment."

Paul distinguishes the wages earned by work from the gift that comes from God's grace. This distinction helps us avoid the trap of thinking we can earn God's pleasure; that he owes us anything. Paul quotes Psalm 32.

> The blessedness of the one to whom God credits righteousness apart from works: Blessed are those whose transgressions are forgiven, whose sins are covered. Blessed is the one whose sin the Lord will never count against them. (Romans 4:6-7)

Paul notes that this blessedness is available to all, using Abraham's faith before he underwent the ritual of circumcision as proof that this sanctity is not restricted to just the Jews.

Abraham's circumcision was a watershed event in his relationship with God. Abram, as he was, responded to God's call years earlier and had been living in obedience to God's will for many years. But the ritual of circumcision separated him from the nations around him so that his descendants became a people peculiar to the LORD.

Likewise, baptism is an external sign of a Christian being separated to God.

> And the father of circumcision to those who not only are of the circumcision, but who also follow in the steps of the faith of our father Abraham which he had while uncircumcised. For the promise to Abraham or to his descendants that he would be heir of the world was not through

the Law, but through the righteousness of
faith. (Romans 4:12-13 NASB)

All this apparent quibbling about Abraham is
important because Paul is preparing his reader for the
idea, to be presented in Romans 7, that the law is not
our friend in our search for personal righteousness and
salvation.

For now, Paul is content to drive this stake in the
ground: "For the law brings about wrath, but where there
is no law, there is also no transgression" (Romans 4:15
NASB).

Remember that Paul opened his letter reporting, "But
because of your stubbornness and your unrepentant heart,
you are storing up wrath against yourself for the day of
God's wrath" (Romans 2:5).

"Therefore, the promise comes by faith, so that it
may be by grace and may be guaranteed to all Abraham's
offspring—not only to those who are of the law but also
to those who have the faith of Abraham. He is the father
of us all" (Romans 4:16).

Abraham put his faith in God, even though he and
Sarah were far passed the age of parenthood, that God
would provide the promised offspring through which his
promises would play out.

> Yet, with respect to the promise of God,
> [Abraham] did not waver in unbelief but
> grew strong in faith, giving glory to God,
> and being fully assured that what God had

> promised, He was able also to perform.
> Therefore it was also credited to him as
> righteousness. (Romans 4:20-22 NASB)

Do you see it? Abraham believed that God *could* do and *would* do what he promised, and Abraham stepped out on that belief. That foundation of faith caused Paul to lift him up as a model for us.

"Jesus asked, 'When the Son of Man comes, will He find faith on the earth?'" (Luke 18:8). What kind of faith will he be looking for?

A Roman centurion asked Jesus to cure his servant (Matthew 8 and Luke 7). As with all such humble requests, Jesus agreed, even though most Jews wouldn't even talk to an officer of that hated occupying empire. In fact, just to enter a Gentile's house carried the probability of contamination, rendering Jesus ritually unclean. But "Jesus said to him, 'I will come and heal him'" (Matthew 8:7).

The centurion's response is memorable.

> "Lord, I do not deserve to have you come
> under my roof. But just say the word, and
> my servant will be healed. For I myself am
> a man under authority, with soldiers under
> me. I tell this one, 'Go,' and he goes; and
> that one, 'Come,' and he comes. I say to my
> servant, 'Do this,' and he does it."

> When Jesus heard this, he was amazed and
> said to those following him, "Truly I tell
> you, I have not found anyone in Israel with
> such great faith." (Matthew 8:8-10)

"[Jesus] was amazed," Matthew reports. Surely not that the centurion had humbly requested a miracle from a Jew. Others had asked and received healing from Jesus. Surely not that the centurion balked at Jesus' offer to come to his house. Jesus understood ritual cleanliness, even if the centurion didn't. He was amazed that this Roman—this Gentile defiler of Jesus' homeland—knew what authority was and recognized it in Jesus.

Do you know how many times the gospels report Jesus being amazed?

Many times others are amazed at the words or actions of Jesus, but only twice the Bible records Jesus himself as amazed. Here in Matthew 18 and in Mark 6:6, when he visited Nazareth, and "He could not do any miracles there, except lay his hands on a few sick people and heal them. He was amazed at their lack of faith." That was not good; here his amazement is positive.

On this occasion, Jesus goes on to say,

> "I say to you that many will come from the
> east and the west, and will take their places
> at the feast with Abraham, Isaac and Jacob
> in the kingdom of heaven. But the subjects
> of the kingdom will be thrown outside, into

> the darkness, where there will be weeping
> and gnashing of teeth." (Matthew 8:11-12)

When Jesus suggests that "subjects of the kingdom" may be thrown out, many of us complacently picture the Jews being evicted to make room for us. Perhaps we should be concerned that it isn't we ourselves being ushered to the door.

Jesus is making an important point: he is looking for followers showing the unquestioned faith the centurion describes, and which the centurion exhibits by acknowledging that Jesus needs only say the word for his servant to be healed..

> Such servants [as the centurion's] we all should be to God; we must go and come, according to the directions of his word and the disposals of his providence. But when the Son of man comes he finds little faith, therefore he finds little fruit. An outward profession may cause us to be called children of the kingdom; but if we rest in that, and have nothing else to show, we shall be cast out.
>
> — Matthew Henry

Is Matthew exaggerating? Was Jesus really amazed? Read on, "Then Jesus said to the centurion, 'Go! Let it be done just as you believed it would.' And his servant was healed at that moment" (Matthew 8:13).

Jesus responded in proportion to what the centurion believed. If Jesus told you, "Let it be done just as you believed it would," what would result? Is your faith meter full or empty? Do you even know?

Will Jesus be amazed at your faith? Gary Garner said, "Those who touch the spirit realm grow in it daily."

Let's follow as Paul unlocks the door to which faith has provided the key.

Study Questions

Chapter 5
Faith Not Works

1. What is faith? Does the faith-versus-works question sound like a chicken-or-the-egg controversy? Why is the distinction important?

2. Do you, like Abraham, believe God can and will do what he promises? How does your daily life reflect your confidence?

3. Will Jesus be amazed by your faith? If Jesus says to you, "Let it be done just as you believed it would," what would happen?

4. What's the problem with earning God's favor by what you do? How do your best efforts count? Or not? How is that the wrong way to achieve righteousness?

5. If salvation were possible by human effort, we would have grounds for boasting, but if it's all by God's grace what is the proper response of the redeemed?

CHAPTER 6

DEAD TO SIN

Romans 4:24 - 6:13

❖

EARLIER WE SPOKE of our need for salvation, sometimes even though we were supposedly saved. Our Salvation Meter shows how we all start life empty, and that's bad. Bad, Paul tells us, because we fail to recognize God as God and think we can be good apart from him; bad because we judge others by the very standards which we break ourselves; and bad because we teach others to violate the laws, too. We explored how God's prevenient grace provides the shed blood of Jesus to atone for our sins. Our sins are forgiven—God has done everything that needed doing—long before we are aware of our miserable condition. We don't earn salvation; it is a gift.

The grace of God is so rich and so full that we might be tempted to gloss over differentiations like these and miss the magnificence that the Holy Spirit revealed through Paul. Not understanding the fullness of what God does for us inhibits our ability to function in the full grace, freedom, and power that he designed for us.

Being saved (justified) only moves the meter off empty. Once you're redeemed, there's "gas" in your tank. That's good. But if we just have our sins forgiven, we keep on sinning. We're saved; we're going to heaven, but we may be missing God's best for us. Are you content to drive around with the "low fuel" light on? The bell reminding you of how perilous your situation remains? No, you want enough gas that you don't need to worry about running out. To mix metaphors, you want enough horsepower to perform whatever task presents itself.

We shouldn't be content to stay just saved, like the people A. W. Tozer called "insurance Christians." These folks believed and were saved, but may not have changed one bit thereafter. Why? Their reasons are as diverse as they are. Some because their churches taught them no better. Some because they were satisfied with going no farther. Some because someone or something blocked their way. Whether through ignorance, indifference, or interference; we shouldn't stop at being saved when God offers so much more.

We may be insurance Christians and not know it. We quote with approval Blaise Pascal about the "god-shaped" hole in our hearts. Pascal was a great religious thinker during the seventeenth century, but in his search for God he did not find certainty. He, like many today, tried to consider this rationally.

This may be how one comes to believe God exists, but it has nothing to do with having faith in God. Augustine said, "That hast made us for thyself, and our heart has no rest till it comes to thee."

Paul has already established that nothing we do saves us. When God looks at us, he sees the shed blood of Jesus instead of our own sin and failure. Over and over through the first four chapters of Romans, Paul talks about our sins (plural) and God's remedy for them. "Jesus our Lord . . . was delivered over because of our transgressions, and was raised because of our justification" (Romans 4:24-25 NASB).

Tozer declares, "Justification and regeneration are not the same. They may be thought apart in theology but they can never be experienced apart in fact; when God *declares* a man righteous He instantly sets about to *make* him righteous."

A transformation must take place. When it doesn't, we have reason to suspect the individual took too much for granted.

Starting in chapter 5 of Romans, Paul writes less about sins (plural) and focuses instead on sin (singular). That grammatical shift suggests something important. When he speaks of our sins, Paul discusses obtaining forgiveness for them: justification. But, to become free from sin—that is, our sin nature—he writes, "In order that, just as Christ was raised from the dead through the glory of the Father, we too may live a new life" (Romans 6:4). Living that new life is what theologians call sanctification. Each of us becoming holy—separated to God.

Our problem is not just that we sin, but that we are sinners. We are bent toward sin. If God forgave all our sins and if we lived a pure life (as if we could), we would still be sinners. Our sins are forgiven; God is no longer our enemy (he never was, but we felt estranged by our sins and guilt—remember guilt?), but that's not the end. If it were, Romans would be a pamphlet instead of the longest epistle. It's not the end because we keep sinning. We keep sinning because we're still sinners.

The word "sinner" rarely occurs in the first four chapters of Romans. Now, Paul tackles our very nature. In fact, he doesn't just call us sinners, but slaves to sin. Chained involuntarily. How? It's hereditary.

We are born into sin as the children of Adam. How so? We participated with Adam and Eve in their sin, just as we participated with Jesus in his crucifixion. Adam was the first man and the first sinner. He is our heritage; we are his descendents.

Instead of facing reality, we excuse ourselves, "Yes, I fall short every now and then, but deep inside I know I'm a good person."

No, you're not.

"Well," you reply, "God knows my heart."

Yes, he does. That's why he had Paul write this letter.

Deep down inside you—we all, in our natural state, are sinners. We want things our way. We want it all. We want it now. And we're willing to lie, cheat and steal (that is, commit sins) to get them.

"But God demonstrates his own love toward us, in that while we were still sinners, Christ died for us" (Romans 5:8 NASB). Sinners; not just sinning. Wallowing in the depths of our arrogance, we didn't even want to be saved. We hadn't confessed, repented, apologized—nothing. We were fit only for destruction. And at that point, Jesus took our sins—took us upon himself and bled and died for us.

> Therefore, just as through one man sin entered into the world, and death through sin, and so death spread to all men, because all sinned—for until the Law sin was in the world, but sin is not imputed when there is no law. Nevertheless death reigned from Adam until Moses, even over those who had not sinned in the likeness of the offense of Adam, who is a type of Him who was to come. (Romans 5:12-14 NASB)

Notice how Paul contrasts the obedience of Jesus with the disobedience of Adam: "For as through the one man's disobedience the many were made sinners, even so through the obedience of the One the many will be made righteous." (Romans 5:19 NASB)

When we first became Christians our sins concerned us but, as we learned that God had already dealt with them, we became aware that our problem goes much deeper.

The problem isn't what we do so much as what we are. We try to be good. We try to obey. We try to be humble. But we fail. In fact, the harder we try, the more difficult we realize the problem is.

Because of the disobedience of one man, we are a different people than God designed us to be. And we, of ourselves, can do nothing to alter the situation. We are sons of Adam and daughters of Eve—not in the happy Narnia sense, but in the fallen sense of being sinners. Each of us is the unwilling offspring of every generation before us, all the way back to the first couple. I'm Adam's son. If Adam had died young, I would not be. Neither would you.

Wait, you say, that's not fair. I wasn't in Eden. I didn't sin. But in a sense you were, and you did. After eating the fruit of the tree of the knowledge of good and evil, Adam and Eve's eyes were opened (Genesis 3:7). They saw themselves as naked. They knew they had disobeyed. They felt guilt. And we, their children, still judge for ourselves. We are in Adam and Eve. And now we bear the sin nature. We can choose good from bad, but we often choose the bad. And there's nothing we can do to undo it.

> "But the free gift is not like the transgression. For if by the transgression of the one the many died, much more did the grace of God and the gift by the grace of the one Man, Jesus Christ, abound to the many." (Romans 5:15 NASB)

In Adam we became heirs to death, in Christ we receive all that is of Christ. Paul discussed how we're in Adam. What does he mean we are "in Christ"?

Hebrews (7:14-17) discusses the priesthood of Jesus being "in the order of Melchizedek." This is not a play on words, but an important principle: in every way, Jesus is superior to those who came before him—both positionally and functionally. Hebrews here addresses how his priesthood exceeds that of Levi.

It stems from Genesis 14 where Abraham gave a tithe to Melchizedek while Levi was still "in Abraham." Similarly, we are "in Adam." The logic may strike you as arcane, but the point is that in Adam all are lost, while in Christ all have hope.

The end of all this is to save us from sin. Paul asks like his rhetorical heckler, "Are we to continue in sin so that grace may increase?" (Romans 6:1 NASB).

No! In Christ, "how shall we who died to sin still live in it?" (Romans 6:2 NASB).

"Died to sin"? What does that mean? Since we were born into sin, we must die to escape it. Only death emancipates us. "All of us who were baptized into Christ Jesus have been baptized into his death" (Romans 6:3 NASB).

How, then, do we get into Christ? Easy. We are in because God put us in. "Because of him [God] that you are in Christ Jesus" (1 Corinthians 1:30). We don't have to get good enough, strong enough, or pure enough. We are in Christ. When Jesus was on the cross we were in him, and when he died, being in him, we all died, too. Paul wrote, "One died for all, and therefore all died" (2 Corinthians 5:14). When Jesus was crucified, all of us were crucified with him.

Watchman Nee illustrates this point by putting a slip of paper into a book. Now, whatever we do to the book—drop it, carry it home with us, mail it to Springfield—happens to the slip of paper, too.

Must we ask God to crucify us? No, it's already happened. The Greek here is in the continuing past sense. Scripture confirms this over and over. "Our old self was crucified with Him" (Romans 6:6 NASB). "I have been crucified with Christ and I no longer live, but Christ lives in me" (Galatians 2:20). "Those who belong to Christ Jesus have crucified the sinful nature with its passions and desires," (Galatians 5:24) or "May I never boast except in the cross of our Lord Jesus Christ, through which the world has been crucified to me, and I to the world" (Galatians 6:14). It's a done deal, my friends. An eternal fact.

Jesus shed his blood to atone for our sins; he died that we might die with him. In his death, he included you and me. Likewise, his resurrection includes you and me.

We referred to Paul's first letter to the Corinthians to establish that we are in Christ. Let's look further into that epistle. 1 Corinthians 15:45 & 47 calls Jesus the last Adam and the second man. "The first man Adam became a living being; the last Adam, a life-giving spirit." And "The first man was of the dust of the earth, the second man from heaven."

As the last Adam, Jesus was the culmination—the conclusion of man as a fallen race. As the second man—or the second type of man—he was head of a new race. First, he took all that was of Adam, and took it upon himself—all the sin, judgment and death that every child of Adam deserves. Then, as the second man, Nee advises us, "having in his death done away with the first man in whom God's purpose was frustrated, [Jesus] rose again as Head of a new race of men, in whom that purpose will at length be fully realized."

Praise God.

Paul continues in Romans 6:5 (NASB), "For if we have become united with Him in the likeness of His death, certainly we shall also be in the likeness of His resurrection." On the cross we were transformed from Adam to Christ.

"Therefore, if anyone is in Christ, he is a new creation; the old has gone, the new has come!" (2 Corinthians 5:17). When we are in Adam, everything that pertains to him involuntarily devolves to us, but if we are in Christ all that is in Christ comes to us by grace. Not by anything we do, but because we believe—because we have faith.

Nee suggests four aspects of Christian life are described in Romans: knowing, reckoning, presenting ourselves and walking. Start with knowing and reckoning. We read in Romans 6:1-11 that the death of Jesus is representative and inclusive. Nee says, "To justify us, Jesus bore our sins on the cross; to sanctify us, he bore us on the cross."

How did you receive forgiveness? By your effort? No, by accepting Jesus as your substitute and his blood as washing away your sins. What did you do then? Did you pray, "Jesus come die for my sins?" No, you praised God for what he had already done. The same principle applies to your deliverance from your sin nature: the work is done.

Don't ask to be crucified with Jesus; don't even ask for him to be crucified again for you. It's done. Rejoice!

"Christ died for us" (Romans 5:8), "Our old self was crucified with Him" (Romans 6:6 NASB), and "We have died with Christ" (Romans 6:8 NASB). How could it be more clear?

Jesus was executed by crucifixion. That's a historical fact. We were crucified with him. That's a spiritual fact. When he died on the cross, you died with him. And, if you believe in the death of Jesus Christ, you can just as surely believe in your own death, too. How do you know? Because you feel it? Because you figured it out? Because you will it to be so? No, because the Word of God tells you so.

Our crucifixion is not accomplished by our will, our effort or our feelings, it is accomplished in us by recognizing the finished work of Calvary. By faith. That's how we are saved.

Man's approach to salvation is to overcome sin by effort. Many of us have tried, and we all failed. That's not God's way. God's way is to remove the sinner. You are powerless to do anything; God has already done it all.

Now we're ready to distinguish between knowing and reckoning.

Everything in Romans 1 – 4 is knowing. Knowing is having our eyes opened to reality. There's no logic, no puzzling it out, no calculation. We know it because we know it ... by divine revelation, if you will. You "see" it in your spirit. A light shines within you, and you see Christ in you and you in Christ. You know it is true because God reveals it to you by his spirit. Once you see it—yes, I understand that not everyone does see it, but once you see it, nothing can shake your assurance in that fact.

Christians come to Christ in many ways, but what is common to all is that somehow at some time, each of us discover who Christ is and what he did for us. Only then Paul can write, "knowing this, that our old self was crucified with *Him,* in order that our body of sin might be done away with, so that we would no longer be slaves to sin" (Romans 6:6 NASB). Do you see that, "Knowing this"? Knowing what? That "we have become united with *Him* in the likeness of His death" (Romans 6:5 NASB). The revelation, then, is not about who we are or what we have done, it's about the finished work of Christ.

Remember Jesus' metaphor of the vine?

> I am the true vine, and my Father is the gardener. He cuts off every branch in me that bears no fruit, while every branch that does bear fruit he prunes so that it will be even more fruitful. You are already clean

Ron Andrea

> because of the word I have spoken to you. Remain in me, as I also remain in you. No branch can bear fruit by itself; it must remain in the vine. Neither can you bear fruit unless you remain in me.
>
> I am the true vine, and My Father is the vinedresser. Every branch in Me that does not bear fruit, He takes away; and every branch that bears fruit, He prunes it so that it may bear more fruit. You are already clean because of the word which I have spoken to you. Abide in Me, and I in you. As the branch cannot bear fruit of itself unless it abides in the vine, so neither can you unless you abide in Me. I am the vine, you are the branches; he who abides in Me and I in him, he bears much fruit, for apart from Me you can do nothing. (John 15:1-5 NASB)

We don't become part of the vine by our own effort either. We are made part of it—grafted on—by his supernatural act. You are in Christ. How? By Christ.

Otherwise, it's as if you're sitting in this room, trying to get into this room. That's absurd, but that's how many of us are striving. You're home free! We should spend less time praying for forgiveness and more time praising for being forgiven. God in times past already included you in Christ. When he died, you died; when he rose, a new you rose. Don't sit there praying to die or to be crucified

62

or resurrected. You are dead. You have a new life. You just need to open your eyes and see that he's already done it all.

Do you know it? "Or do you not know that all of us who have been baptized into Christ Jesus have been baptized into His death?" (Romans 6:3 NASB).

Okay, we know we were crucified with Christ. (This is another of those done-in-the-past-continuing-forever Greek verb tenses.) Since we know we're dead, "Even so consider yourselves to be dead to sin, but alive to God in Christ Jesus" (Romans 6:11 NASB). (Some translations actually use the word "reckon" instead of "consider.")

Until we know, there can be no reckoning. If we don't know—in that solid, unchangeable way I discussed before—there's no foundation for you to determine where you stand now. In fact, if you don't know you are dead in Christ, all your reckoning, thinking, and mental gymnastics will only confuse you.

The secret of reckoning is revelation. I don't reckon myself dead; I am dead. I don't reckon toward death; I reckon from death. The words translated as "reckon," "count" or "consider" have nothing to do with speculative thinking. They are the Greek words for doing accounts … bookkeeping. Adding numbers. If one thing is true in both heaven and on earth, and even in hell, it's that one plus one equals two. (It's axiomatic. There's no proving that, you just know it.)

We can reckon ourselves dead to sin because we are, in fact, dead.

The first four chapters of Romans are about faith. Faith, faith and more faith. We are justified by faith. Faith is my acceptance of God's fact. It's based on what has already happened. Now Paul starts talking about reckoning. If it's based on the facts that we know, then we can reckon in good hope. What relates to the future is hope. "For in this hope we were saved" (Romans 8:24).

When I have faith in my death, then I can believe that in Christ I am already crucified. In Romans 3 we saw that Jesus bore our sins and died for our forgiveness. In Romans 6 we see ourselves included in the death through which he secured our deliverance. Reckoning, based on what we know, joins faith. We look toward the future secure that as one plus one equals two, even as solidly we are dead to sin. Otherwise we're like folks who view all calculations with uncertainty.

We need to be careful here. Paul said we were dead to sin, not that sin doesn't still exist or that it doesn't attract us or even that we can't sin.

God's method for dealing with sins we committed is direct; he blots them out by means of the shed blood of Jesus. His method for dealing with the power of sin is more subtle; he does not remove the sin, but the sinner. Paul tells us, "Do not go on presenting the members of your body to sin *as* instruments of unrighteousness; but present yourselves to God as those alive from the dead, and your members *as* instruments of righteousness to God" (Romans 6:13 NASB).

In that way we are delivered from the power of sin, in line with Paul's advise in Romans 6:11 that we should "consider (as in "reckon") yourselves dead to sin but alive to God in Christ Jesus." The life of Christ planted in us does not, by its nature, sin. It's the difference between the history and the nature of a thing. What is in Christ cannot sin, but what is in Adam can and will.

So, which facts are you going to believe? On what basis will you reckon? The tangible facts of every day experience or the Word of God that is at work in our salvation?

Both are true in their way. It's a matter of our making real in our lives—in the making of our history—what is true in divine fact. Hebrews 11:1 reports, "Now faith is being sure of what we hope for and certain of what we do not see." What does that mean? "Being sure" is not static: a thing. No, the Greek describes an action. There's a sense of doing. J. N. Darby translates Hebrews 11:1 as, "Faith is the substantiating of things hoped for." Meaning that faith actively brings the things hoped of into being. Hebrews 11 then lists men who acted on that faith, serving God.

If I am blind, I cannot see color. If I'm deaf, I cannot hear music. Color and music are nonetheless real. Likewise, we're considering things which, though they are not seen, are eternal and therefore real. In 2 Corinthians 4:18 Paul wrote "what is seen is temporary, but what is unseen is eternal." Life—all of nature—is subject to decay. It's called entropy. Reckoning makes things—things hoped for in Christ—real in faith. Faith substantiates to me the things of Christ. As real things, they then enter my experience.

Remember, we are dealing here with facts, not promises. These things are real whether we believe them or not. Jesus said, "your word is truth" (John 17:17). If we do not believe the facts of the cross, they remain real, but they are valueless to us. Faith is not needed to make them real, but faith substantiates them and makes them real in our experience.

Corrie ten Boom's family was imprisoned by the Nazis during the Second World War for hiding Jews in their home in Haarlem. Years later she met one of the guards of Ravensbruck prison. The former guard approached her and asked forgiveness. Corrie recounts her reaction (in *The Hiding Place*) as follows:

> And I stood there — I whose sins had every day to be forgiven — and could not. Betsie had died in that place — could he erase her slow terrible death simply for the asking?
>
> It could not have been many seconds that he stood there, hand held out, but to me it seemed hours as I wrestled with the most difficult thing I had ever had to do.
>
> For I had to do it — I knew that. The message that God forgives has a prior condition: that we forgive those who have

injured us. "If you do not forgive men their trespasses," Jesus says, "neither will your Father in heaven forgive your trespasses."

And still I stood there with the coldness clutching my heart. But forgiveness is not an emotion — I knew that too. Forgiveness is an act of the will, and the will can function regardless of the temperature of the heart. "Jesus, help me!" I prayed silently. "I can lift my hand, I can do that much. You supply the feeling."

And so woodenly, mechanically, I thrust my hand into the one stretched out to me. And as I did, an incredible thing took place. The current started in my shoulder, raced down my arm, sprang into our joined hands. And then this healing warmth seemed to flood my whole being, bringing tears to my eyes.

"I forgive you, brother!" I cried. "With all my heart!"

For a long moment we grasped each other's hands, the former guard and the former prisoner. I had never known God's love so intensely as I did then.

Corrie's forgiveness was not real in that situation until she thrust her hand into his. She substantiated God's love to that former guard and in her own heart when she moved. She was saved; she just wasn't experiencing it. What are you experiencing?

Our faith becomes real only when we start living it.

Study Questions

Chapter 6
Dead to Sin

1. How do you "walk in newness of life?" If your sins can be forgiven, but you still be a sinner, what are you to do? How does one get free from his or her sin nature?

2. Isn't being able to judge between good and evil good? Why would God withhold it from us? Analyze your response.

3. Have you been united with Christ in his death? Do you know it? Do you reckon yourself dead to sin? Do you experience that truth? Participate in it?

4. Are you living God's forgiveness? What are you doing to be secure in your relationship with God? Why is it important to be secure?

5. How does God's grace make a difference in your everyday life? Why is grace such a hard concept to accept?

CHAPTER 7

Re-Born

Romans 6:14 - 23

◆

WE MUST BELIEVE God, no matter how convincing Satan's arguments seem. The devil is a liar (John 8:44). A skillful liar. He's had lots of practice. He knows how to mislead and confuse. Look what he did to Eve (Genesis 3:1-7), and tried to do to Jesus (Matthew 4:1-11). But "We walk by faith, not by sight" (2 Corinthians 5:7).

Temptation is the urge to take our eyes off Jesus, to judge for ourselves what's right and what's wrong, to take into account how things appear. If we resort to our senses to determine what's true, we fall into Satan's trap because he can surely manipulate appearances. But if we refuse to accept anything that contradicts God's Word and keep our faith in God alone, Satan's lies unravel and our experience increasingly matches that Word. Faith substantiates our hope.

Whether I feel that way or not, I am dead with Christ. "One died for all, and therefore all died" (2 Corinthians 5:14). In Christ we see real righteousness, real holiness, real resurrection life—for us. That's why Paul writes in Galatians 4:19, "I am again in the pains of childbirth until Christ is formed in you." Faith is always substantiating eternal facts—eternal truth.

We are not dead in ourselves. No, we are dead in Christ. Jesus said, "Remain in me, as I also remain in you" (John 15:4). God has done the work, not we as individuals. We can't experience anything spiritual separate from him. What we call *our* experience is only our entering into his history and his experience.

Some Christians seek experiences for their own sake—speaking in tongues or healing or miracles. Tozer calls them "fireworks Christians." Their eyes are on the fireworks, not on Christ. Churches where whooping and hollering beats out listening to the still, small voice of God. Watchman Nee wrote, "Every true spiritual experience means that we have discovered a certain fact about Christ, and have entered into that [fact]."

The facts of Christ are the foundation of our experience. God does not give us experiences, so much as we enter into what God has already done. We do not, as Christians, have a history separate from God. Not even eternal life. "He who has the Son has life; he who does not have the Son of God does not have life" (1 John 5:12).

Instead we should say, "God has put me into Christ, and therefore all that is true of him is true of me. I will abide in him." Abide is God's command. That is the way of deliverance. He promises "Abide in me, and I in you" (John 15:4 NASB). If we do the first, he will do the second.

Suppose you're sitting at home and evening comes, you do not look at the light and pray for it to come on. You do not lay hands on the bulb or prophesy to it. No, you get up, go to the switch—even if it's on the wall across the room—and you turn on the current. You know the power is there. You act in faith, and the power flows. Guess who is our spiritual power source? God. Go to him. Fix your attention on Christ. "But we all ... beholding ... glory of the Lord, are being transformed into the same image" (2 Corinthians 3:18 NASB). "He who abides in Me and I in him, he bears much fruit, for apart from Me you can do nothing" (John 15:5 NASB).

How do we abide? God's work puts you there [in Christ], and he has done it. Now your job is to stay there. Don't wander off.

"For sin shall not be master over you, for you are not under law but under grace" (Romans 6:14 NASB). Then why does Paul keep harping on staying free from the law of sin? For the very obvious reason that we can move ourselves out from under the umbrella of God's grace. Not God—heaven knows, not Satan—but you and I by the way we think, feel and act. *We* can remove ourselves from God's grace.

To understand how this works, let's make another small digression. We Christians know that the kingdom of this world is not the kingdom of God. Jesus said, "My kingdom is not of this world. If it were, my servants would fight to prevent my arrest by the Jewish leaders. But now my kingdom is from another place" (John 18:36). Paul wrote to the Colossians (1:17) "For by him all things were created: things in heaven and on earth, visible and invisible, whether thrones or powers or rulers or authorities; all things were created by him and for him."

But Satan, working through man's flesh, set up an alternate kingdom which he dominates. John 12:13 labels him "the prince of this world." Under Satan's rule, the original creation degenerated into the old creation or old kingdom. In Christ, God is bringing in a new kingdom. Which are we part of? "[God] has rescued us from the dominion of darkness and brought us into the kingdom of the Son he loves" (Colossians 1:12).

To bring us into the new kingdom God must make us new creatures. "That which is born of the flesh is flesh, and that which is born of the Spirit is spirit" (John 3:6 NASB), and "flesh and blood cannot inherit the kingdom of God, nor does the perishable inherit the imperishable" (1 Corinthians 15:50). Our fitness for the new kingdom is based on which creation we are part of. If we are flesh, we are of the old kingdom and cannot enter the new. We can't even bring anything from the old creation into the new. He had to kill us on the cross and raise us from the grave. "If anyone is in Christ, he is a new creation; the old has gone, the new has come!" (2 Corinthians 5:17).

By the cross God ended the old, and by the resurrection he made us anew. "Therefore we have been buried with Him through baptism into death, so that as Christ was raised from the dead through the glory of the Father, so we too might walk in newness of life" (Romans 6:4 NASB). By the cross God wiped out everything that was not of him; by the resurrection he started the new creation.

So, we have two worlds before us: the old, dominated by Satan; and the new, under the dominion of God. As long as you belong to the old creation, you—and everything else in it—are under the sentence of death. Nothing from Adam can go beyond the cross. The cross is our point of escape from the kingdom of death. Everything not of God dies, including us.

But God provides a means of escape.

> Do you not know that all of us who have been baptized into Christ Jesus have been baptized into His death? Therefore we have been buried with Him through baptism into death, so that as Christ was raised from the dead through the glory of the Father, so we too might walk in newness of life. (Romans 6:3-4 NASB)

Jesus said, "Whoever believes and is baptized will be saved" (Mark 16:16). By baptism we die to the old creation and are born into the new. You, and your old world, spiritually die when you go down into the water; you come up a new creation into a new world. Baptism is not just a question of water or of how it is applied; it is of you identifying yourself with the death and resurrection of Christ.

Baptism symbolizes our burial with Christ. Who is buried? The living? No, the dead. When I ask for baptism, I declare myself dead, unfit for anything except burial. Not that I am trying to die. I'm recognizing that I already died. Baptism is a conscious and visible break with the old me. That's why Paul asked, "How shall we who died to sin still live in it?" (Romans 6:2 NASB), and answers, "If we have become united with *Him* in the likeness of His death, certainly we shall also be *in the likeness* of His resurrection" (Romans 6:5 NASB).

Notice the difference. In baptism: I join him in his death, but I don't enter his resurrection, it enters me. That phrase in Romans 6:5 "united with Him" is not a simple joining. It means planted together—grafted together. In death, I am in Christ; in resurrection, Christ is in me. How? I don't know. But Jesus assures us, "The wind blows wherever it pleases. You hear its sound, but you cannot tell where it comes from or where it is going. So it is with everyone born of the Spirit" (John 3:8).

This is the new birth. God has done it all. Not that my natural life has changed, but a new, altogether divine life has begun in me. Baptism is your public testimony. Paul explains in Romans 10:9, "If you confess with your mouth, 'Jesus is Lord,' and believe in your heart that

God raised him from the dead, you will be saved," with 10:10, "For with the heart a person believes, resulting in righteousness, and with the mouth he confesses, resulting in salvation."

If you haven't been baptized, I suggest you talk to your pastor. If you haven't got a pastor, find one. Soon.

Don't put off baptism or anything else that gets you closer to God. He's doing all sorts of neat stuff that you want to be a part of. Don't put this off until tomorrow. Not just because you may die before then, but because you'll miss twenty-four hours of God's best for you.

We discussed knowing and reckoning, now consider "presenting"—as in, offering ourselves to the Lord. Paul writes,

> Therefore do not let sin reign in your mortal body so that you obey its lusts, and do not go on presenting the members of your body to sin *as* instruments of unrighteousness; but present yourselves to God as those alive from the dead, and your members *as* instruments of righteousness to God. (Romans 6:12-13 NASB)

Presenting. Get it?

"Present yourselves to God as those alive from the dead," Paul writes. You, died and resurrected, are now ready to present your members to God. Not as some casual toss-a-dollar-in-the-plate offering, but as a consecration.

As the high priest's garments were inscribed: "Holy to the LORD" (Exodus 28:36).

What is this kind of presenting? Not merely becoming holy by rooting out the sin within us. Oh, no, it's being separated unto God. Separated from our old life, from our old habits, separated from the world. We must consciously and conscientiously make ourselves altogether his.

This is a definite thing; as definite as knowing and reckoning. Consecrating ourselves, not to being good, not to Christian work, not belonging to the church, but consecrating ourselves to the will of the Lord.

Do you see the difference?

As a Christian, our pathway—what Paul called our "course" in 2 Timothy 4:7 is set by God. We have but one life to live and we are free to live it as we please, but if we seek to map out our own course our life will never glorify God.

Whose will are you following? Your will or God's will?

Giving myself to God must be my initial, fundamental act once I am in God. I have to take my hands off the steering wheel of my life and entrust it to him. If I belong to God, then I can't be steering. I must acknowledge his ownership and his authority over everything in and about me. That is presenting ourselves to God: knowing that we are no longer our own. Every time I grab the steering wheel—even to do what seems right in my eyes—I return to the kingdom of this world.

So, where are we? Through the blood you have died to your sins. Through the cross you have been born a new creature. With Romans 6, we must have moved to the best of all possible worlds, right? Actually, no. We're further along than many Christians. It's good, but it isn't all. There's more.

Look at Romans 8:28 (NASB). "And we know that God causes all things to work together for good to those who love God, to those who are called according to His purpose." Many "entitlement Christians" cite this verse as proof that God is some sort of supernatural Santa Claus. Nothing could be further from the truth.

God is working in all things for the good of those that love him, but the good he's working for is good as he, not we, defines it. It's kingdom good. Jesus tells us, "But seek first His kingdom and his righteousness, and all these things will be added to you" (Matthew 6:33 NASB). Not going to God for what we can get, whether prosperity or security or even his love. We move into the sweet spot of God's will only when we seek him for who he is and obey him.

For now we can be content that God is working everything for good. We can trust him to do what's right for us and to us, even if we don't understand and can't see the light at the end of the tunnel. "A man's steps are directed by the LORD. How then can anyone understand his own way?" (Proverbs 20:24).

Every day, every night I must offer myself to God. "Trust and obey, for there's no other way /to be happy in Jesus, but to trust and obey." (John H. Sammis, 1887)

As consecrated to God, we are finally off the "low fuel" warning and into the sweetness of God's will and his plan for our lives. The needle of our gas gauge has moved well above empty.

Study Questions

Chapter 7
Re-Born

1. How does your spiritual experience enter the facts of Christ? How do you abide in him?
2. Which creation are you part of? Are you in Christ through baptism, and is Christ in you through the resurrection?
3. How have you presented yourself to God? How have you separated yourself from the world and who you were?
4. Do you seek God for who he is, not for what he can do for you? What's wrong with that?
5. Where is your greatest struggle: understanding God's salvation truths, really being convinced by those truths, or choosing to live them out?

CHAPTER 8

WRETCHED

Romans 7

◆

WHEN YOU READ Romans straight through, you notice the apparent disconnect between chapters six, seven and eight. At first glance the seventh chapter of Romans seems like a mistake or out of place. Paul has taken us from "all have sinned" through "cleansed by the blood" through "dead (crucified) to sin" to "holy to the Lord." Suddenly, he declares,

"What a wretched man I am!" (Romans 7:24). Forgiven. Free from the sins I've committed, but still apparently in bondage to the law of sin. "Nothing good lives in me, that is, in my sinful nature" (Romans 7:18). (Notice also the text has shifted from third person past tense, to first person present tense. From "he was" to "I am." Paul's talking about himself, right then. He's baring his soul.) Further along, he states, "Those controlled by the sinful nature cannot please God" (Romans 8:8).

What's happening? Why this apparent digression? Maybe Paul (and the Holy Spirit) know the true state of our hearts. Declaring the transformation Paul described in the previous chapters is not the same as actually experiencing it. We should have plenty of gas in our tank, but our "low fuel" warning is ringing.

Many Christians—many of us—are truly saved yet still bound by sin. There's a sea of difference between just being saved and being holy. Holiness is the evidence of grace at work in our lives. Even if we look holy, most of us know—like Paul—that it's an act. That's because holiness isn't just a matter of works, it's a matter of the ruling principle of our lives.

It's the difference between the fairy tale Bible many modern Christians apparently believe in and the real Bible. Paul is being real. Life doesn't magically become wonderful just because we believe in Jesus. It's not all sunshine and daisies just because we join God's team. This is real life. This is where God meets us.

We ended the last chapter with the idea of presenting ourselves to God. Paul picks up there, "Therefore, my brethren, you also were made to die to the Law through the body of Christ ... in order that we might bear fruit for God" (Romans 7:4 NASB).

That seems reasonable: now that I'm dedicated to God, I should want to discover his will and do it. I thought I could do it. I thought I'd like it.

It turns out that I can't and I don't.

Did I know? Yes, I know that Jesus shed his blood and died for me. I was saved—justified. Did I reckon? Yes, I reckoned myself dead to sin. Have I withdrawn presenting myself to God? No, I consecrated myself. I still mean it. Then what's the matter?

The more I try, the more I fail. Paul reports, "For I know that nothing good dwells in me, that is, in my flesh; for the willing is present in me, but the doing of the good is not. For the good that I want, I do not do, but I practice the very evil that I do not want" (Romans 7:18-19 NASB).

What happened? I understood, agreed and tried to follow Paul's assertions through chapter 6. Make no mistake: the death of Jesus is sufficient—Romans 6:14 (NASB) is operative: "For sin shall not be master over you, for you are not under law but under grace."

What went wrong? Grace means God did something for me; law in this situation means I'm still trying to do something for God. God has certain holy and righteous demands. Deliverance from the law means that God no longer requires that from me, but he provides it himself. The trouble is, we keep trying to please God the old way, and do you know what happens? As soon as we start trying to please God the old way, we place ourselves *back under the law*.

The fault doesn't lie with the law; the fault lies with us. The law's demands aren't unjust; I just can't meet them. Jamie Thompson said, "The law is the light in a dark room that shows you where the dirt is, but it is not the broom that cleans it up. The law doesn't clean us up, for that Jesus had to die."

I keep trying on my own. I think I'm a rather decent fellow; but, as soon as you expect me to actually do something, my sinfulness is revealed. And I try to fix it. God knows who I am; he knows that I'm full of sin; he knows I can't do anything about it. The trouble is: I don't know it. We say we know it, but we don't.

Jesus warned us in the Sermon on the Mount (Matthew 5 - 7) that his standards are much higher than those of the law. He discusses murder and adultery, but it extends all across the law. "Do not covet" means "do not desire." But I'm a big ball of desires. "Do not bear false witness" doesn't just mean don't lie, but also don't deceive. And I'm a faker from head to toe. What do I do every Sunday morning? I fix my hair, brush my teeth, shine my shoes, dress in my finest clothes, carry my biggest Bible, smile big and pretend that I've got it all together. Baloney!

Ask yourself: did you dress last Sunday morning to please God, or considering what others would think of you? He's not fooled. He sees inside!

The more I try to keep the law, the more my inability becomes obvious. The law proves our weakness. But we're so conceited that God must prove our weakness to us. Until at last, with Paul, we confess, "For I know that nothing good dwells in me" (7:18 NASB). Only then has the law served its purpose. It has brought me to the foot of the cross. Again.

In Romans 6 we learned how we were delivered from sin, pictured as a slave and his master. In Romans 7, we learn that we must be delivered from the law through the picture of a wife and two husbands. Paul first explains how the woman's bond to one man can only be broken by death.

> Or do you not know, brethren ... that the law has jurisdiction over a person as long as he lives? For the married woman is bound by law to her husband while he is living; but if her husband dies, she is released from the law concerning the husband. So then, if while her husband is living she is joined to another man, she shall be called an adulteress; but if her husband dies, she is free from the law, so that she is not an adulteress though she is joined to another man. (Romans 7:1-3 NASB)

Assuming she doesn't want to commit murder, how does she get free to marry the second man? Paul's answer is surprising: She—not he—must die.

The first husband is the law, the second husband is Christ, and you are the woman. The law requires much but doesn't help; Christ demands even more but he helps us carry the burden. In fact, he fulfills it for us.

The law will continue for eternity, therefore the only way for us to be free of it is to die. "Therefore, my brethren, you also were made to die to the Law through the body of Christ, so that you might be joined to another, to Him who was raised from the dead" (Romans 7:4 NASB).

Exactly the same principle delivers us from the law as delivered us from our sin nature: I die. Paul said, "You also were made to die to the Law through the body of Christ" (Romans 7:4 NASB). But even as we died with Christ, so we rose with him. So that we are "dead to the law" but alive unto God. To what end? "In order that we might bear fruit for God" (Romans 7:4 NASB).

The law of God is not annulled; it is fulfilled. Like the widow who re-marries. She now possesses her new husband's name and his possessions. All that is Christ's belongs to us.

Christ now works in me what is pleasing to God. That's why Paul admonishes us, "Work out your salvation with fear and trembling, for it is God who works in you to will and to act according to his good purpose" (Philippians 2:12-13). Do you get it? Not that we become lawless, but that we quit trying to fulfill it of ourselves. "It is God who works in you." Trying with your own strength, you leave no room for God. By your effort, you strive and fail. Just as Paul did. (And if Paul can't make it, who can?) Instead, we should let go and trust God to know and do his will in us.

God's requirements aren't changed; of ourselves, we're not meeting them. A drowning man is so desperate that he fights the one trying to save him. Often he can't be saved until he's so exhausted he gives up. We're drowning. God is waiting for us to give up. He has condemned the old creation to the cross. "The flesh profits nothing" (John

6:63). It is fit only for death. So, let it die. By our striving we deny that the cross is totally sufficient.

The "wretched man" of Romans 7:24 causes his own troubles because he tries to fulfill the law of himself. He tries; he fails. He resolves to try harder, but he still fails. We think God asks us to keep the law. No, he wants us to die to it. In Romans 6 we died to sin, now we must die to self. We must trust in Christ alone. "Who will set me free from the body of this death?" Paul asks, and answers. "Thanks be to God through Jesus Christ our Lord!" (Romans 7:24-25 NASB).

How did we obtain forgiveness of sins? Bible reading? Praying? Tithing? No. We believed what Jesus did for us. How were we delivered from sin? The same way.

In both cases, we must depend on him alone. We know that justification is ours through the completed work of Jesus, but somehow we think sanctification depends on our own efforts. "It is finished," Jesus said (John 19:30). He did everything on the cross. "It is God who works in you" (Philippians 2:7).

What is our correct response? How 'bout "Thank you"?

Praise him; worship him. He did all the work, why not give him all the glory? Then what, should we just go our way doing as we please? You know better. Only now, prepared by Romans 7, can we understand what Paul writes in Romans 8. For now we can finally talk about the law of the Spirit of Life. Earlier, we discussed (Romans 5:12 to 6:23) our being "in Adam" and "in Christ." And now (Romans 7:1 to 8:39) we have the opposition of being "in the flesh" and "in the Spirit."

We think it is enough to be "in Christ" but we must also learn to walk "in the Spirit."

Living in the flesh is acting out of myself, as in Adam. I still have the full capacity to sin. Therefore I must learn to walk in the Spirit. In Christ my old man was crucified and is now "blessed … in the heavenly realms with every spiritual blessing in Christ" (Ephesians 1:3). But, if I'm not living in the Spirit, what is true of Christ is not expressed in me. What does that mean? What is objectively true—that I am in Christ—must be made subjectively evident. In my life.

Not only am I in Christ, but Christ is in me. But Christ manifests himself not in terms of flesh but of spirit. Otherwise, what I experience is based on my will and my strength, as if I were still in Adam. Sound familiar?

I must learn to live in the Spirit. I must learn to trust the Holy Spirit to do in me what I cannot do myself. Each time I face a challenge, I must look to Jesus to do in me what he requires of me. Completely different from how I've been living. Not trying, but trusting. Not struggling, but resting in him. As Moses said, "Stand firm and you will see the deliverance the LORD will bring you today" (Exodus 14:13).

How's that work? Have you ever had to do something you detested? Perhaps to visit someone who you didn't really like, or worse who didn't like you. All your past meetings were stressful and aggravating. But this time you leave the relationship with God, you pray before meeting that

Living in the Spirit

person. You pray that God's will be done, not that things go well for you. And, then what? You go and you don't feel so irritated. Oh, your acquaintance didn't act differently, you just didn't feel the attack. Could it be that the Holy Spirit carried you through where your natural actions, even trying to be patient, would have increased the tension?

Tony Fisher reminds us that our thought life can lead us away from God and into sin. What we expose ourselves to predisposes us to sin, even though it may not be sinful in itself. It may be as innocuous as food or clothes, but it may lead us to coveting, gluttony, lust, or murder. Remember, Jesus tells us that being angry is as unacceptable as murder.

> You have heard that the ancients were told, 'You shall not commit murder' and 'Whoever commits murder shall be liable to the court.' But I say to you that everyone who is angry with his brother shall be guilty before the court; and whoever says to his brother, 'You good-for-nothing,' shall be guilty before the supreme court; and whoever says, 'You fool,' shall be guilty enough to go into the fiery hell. (Matthew 5:21-22 NASB)

When the Holy Spirit is in control, we don't need to strain.

Wouldn't it be nice if that happened all the time? Why doesn't it? Maybe the object of temptation is not to get us to sin, so much as to get us to do something of ourselves? We think we have a vote. But in the very thought of deciding for ourselves, we mutiny against God's rule. Once we move out of the Spirit and into the flesh, Satan has won even if we don't do anything overtly wrong.

"For I know that nothing good dwells in me, that is, in my flesh" (Romans 7:18). My flesh—my old self—is the root of my troubles. Short of suicide, what am I to do? Nothing, praise God. It was done for you when you died in Christ. Remember the widow? "Though self is not dead, you are indeed dead to self," Andrew Murray declares. "Your death in Christ has freed you completely from the control of self: it has no power over you, except as you, in ignorance or unwatchfulness or unbelief, consent to yield to its usurped authority."

How then should we act? Divine victory is based on us depending on Christ, not on ourselves. Paul warns us, "For the sinful nature desires what is contrary to the Spirit, and the Spirit what is contrary to the sinful nature. They are in conflict with each other, so that you do not do what you want" (Galatians 5:17). Notice that last phrase: "so you don't do what you want." Why not? Because it's of the flesh: the sinful nature. That's what we would do "naturally". How many of us excuse our sin with "That's the way God made me"? No, that's a flag that you're in rebellion. Instead, we are to "live by the Spirit, and you will not gratify the desires of the sinful nature" (Galatians 5:16).

Victory lies in Christ. Trust him. Nee summarizes this as, "The cross has been given to procure salvation for us; the Spirit has been given to produce salvation in us." Paul wrote, "I no longer live, but Christ lives in me" (Galatians 2:20). The life we should now live is the life of Christ alone.

Christianity is not a changed life; it's an exchanged life. "I no longer live, but Christ lives in me." Christ's life is reproduced in us.

Francis Frangipane suggests, "It is not what we do for the Lord but what we become to Him that matters. It is this inner surrender of the heart, this deliberate turning of our soul Godward, that defines our true progress. Becoming like Jesus is why we exist."

"Regeneration means that the life of Christ is planted in us by the Holy Spirit at our new birth," wrote Nee. "Reproduction goes further: it means that the new life grows and becomes manifest in us, until the very likeness of Christ begins to be reproduced in our lives."

Have you ever been in a situation so bad you wanted to scream or tear out your hair? Do you think you needed patience? No, you didn't need patience, you needed Christ. God does not give patience or humility or love as separate gifts. He has only one gift, his son Jesus Christ.

John wrote, "God has given us eternal life, and this life is in his Son. He who has the Son has life; he who does not have the Son of God does not have life" (1 John 5:11-12). Likewise, Paul writes, "the free gift of God is eternal life in Christ Jesus our Lord" (Romans 6:23 NASB).

There's a big difference between Christian virtue and Christ. In fact, Hans-Werner Bartsch points out that our struggle is not like some Stoic willing good but doing evil but the wrestling of the Christian who is not living up to the grace he has received—our "continued temptation of self-assertion through [our] deeds." Even our good deeds. "Christ Jesus, who has become for us wisdom from God—that is, our righteousness, holiness and redemption." (1 Corinthians 1:30).

Sanctification is not holiness. Sanctification is the fruit of holiness. Holiness is our Lord Jesus Christ. Him living in us separates us from the world; that is how we are sanctified. Andrew Murray told us, "Conformity in Him; that's holiness."

God has one always sufficient answer: his son Jesus Christ. The only sense in which we grow is growing in grace, and grace is God doing something for us. Christ dwells in each of us who believe, but we must learn to trust him in each particular of our lives. Instead of trying, we should be trusting. "Lord, I can't do it; therefore I will not try to do it. From now on I will trust you for that." This is not passivity; it is actively trusting—drawing life from him, letting him live his life in us.

Why does Paul go on and on about his failures? Surely he was one of the most sanctified men then alive. But he kept falling back into his flesh. And he knew it separated him from God. Back sliding, my friends, undoes the connection. Why else do so many healed and liberated people not stay healed and liberated? Because they moved out of faith and back into flesh. Back to their soulish desires. Paul recognized the danger; we should, too.

Look at Hebrews 4:6 (NASB): "Therefore, since it remains for some to enter it, and those who formerly had good news preached to them failed to enter because of disobedience."

The last lesson we should learn from Romans 7 is that we can't expect to live in the higher levels of the spirit if we aren't walking in the lower levels. Justification and sanctification are foundational. If we're not saved, of course, nothing else can happen, other than we expend a lot of energy posing. Well, that's true of walking in the spirit. This is not meant as a condemnation, but as an instruction.

When Paul felt lost, what did he do? (Romans 7:24-25) He returned to the foundation of his salvation: Jesus Christ our Lord.

Like Paul, we should thank God, he has already freed us. Let Jesus' Spirit lift you to freedom and victory.

"Where Jesus Christ is glorified, the Holy Spirit comes," wrote A. W. Tozer.

Study Questions

Chapter 8
Wretched

1. Are you saved but still bound by sin? Are you, like Paul, wretched? Is there evidence that grace is working in your life?

2. Do you want to do God's will? Are you trying to do something for God, or are you letting God do something through you?

3. In what ways are you dead to the law and alive to Christ? Why is the cross sufficient for you?

4. Is the likeness of Christ being reproduced in you? How are you a reflection of Christ?

5. Were you healed and liberated, but are now suffering again? Did you move back into trying to save yourself? Why?

6. Giving in to sinful desires won't please God or hasten the righteous life He requires, but how effective is legalism in fighting the flesh?

7. Just how deadly is sin in your life? How do you acknowledge and deal with it?

CHAPTER 9

Spirit Poured Out

Romans 8

◆

PAUL NOW MOVES to the heart of his message. In many ways these thirty-nine verses are not just the heart of Romans but the heart of the good news of Jesus Christ. Jesus did not just save us for heaven after we die; Jesus opened the door for us to live new, rewarding lives starting here and now. Countless Christians quote verses snatched from this chapter, not realizing the sublime whole of Paul's summation.

Before going further, read Romans 8 in its entirety.

Note that he starts with the word "therefore." This means that what he's about to write is the logical conclusion of what he has just written. Remember reckoning? We're only halfway through the book of Romans, but we are at the focal point of Paul's message.

"Therefore, there is now no condemnation for those who are in Christ Jesus. For the law of the Spirit of life in Christ Jesus has set you free from the law of sin and of death" (Romans 8:1-2 NASB). Based on all he wrote previously in his letter, Paul now concludes his argument.

God saves us from our sin; God also makes it possible for us to be reborn. How? The former through the life, death and resurrection of Jesus; the latter through the outpouring and the indwelling of his Spirit.

> For what the Law could not do, weak as it was through the flesh, God did: sending His own Son in the likeness of sinful flesh and as an offering for sin, He condemned sin in the flesh, so that the requirement of the Law might be fulfilled in us, who do not walk according to the flesh but according to the Spirit. (Romans 8:3-4 NASB)

The Holy Spirit is barely mentioned in the first seven chapters of Romans. In chapter eight the Spirit is identified twenty times. That is not mere literary convention. It is by and through the Holy Spirit that believers experience newness of life.

There are two kinds of condemnation: God's and mine. The blood of Christ assures us we are not condemned before God, but I still condemn myself. Remember guilt? The condemnation Paul describes in chapter 7 is very real. But, as I learn to live by Christ, I become free of self-condemnation. "The mind controlled by the Spirit is life and peace" (Romans 8:6), and it becomes my experience as I learn to walk in the Spirit. Remember substantiating?

Paul writes, "I can do everything through him who gives me strength" (Philippians 4:13). How? "For the law of the Spirit of life in Christ Jesus has set you free from the law of sin and of death" (Romans 8:2 NASB). How? The same way a natural law like gravity is overcome, by the intervention of another, stronger force. In this case, the law of the Spirit of life.

We go wrong depending on ourselves. Even forgiven—even filled with the Holy Spirit—we are trying to live by our own willpower or strength or intelligence. It doesn't work. God already acted on our behalf. Romans 6:23 says, "the gift of God is eternal life in Christ Jesus our Lord." And Romans 8:2 says "the law of the Spirit of life [has] set me free."

This is not a new gift; it's just a new revelation of what we already have. "Set me free" is past tense. If we really see that and put our faith in him, we wouldn't need to undergo the valley of despair described in Romans 7. At least not repeatedly. If we let go of our will and trust him, we don't fall to the ground. We fall into the arms of the law of the Spirit of life. God has not only given us life but also the law of life.

Should we not pray and read the Bible then? Of course, we should. But not out of some legalistic obligation but from a hunger for God's presence and God's word.

The Bible, after all, is our measuring stick to warn us if the wonderful new revelation we've gotten is not from God. "All Scripture is God-breathed and is useful for teaching, rebuking, correcting and training in righteousness" (2 Timothy 3:16). As we live in and internalize the new law, we can be less conscious of the old. We are not forcing ourselves to be what we naturally aren't. "Consider the lilies … they grow," Jesus said (Luke 12:27). And so shall we.

In Romans 8, we reach Nee's fourth principle of Romans: learning to walk after the Spirit. Listen to Paul.

> For what the Law could not do, weak as it was through the flesh, God did … in us, who do not walk according to the flesh but according to the Spirit. (Romans 8:3-4 NASB)

What Jesus did *for* us previously, the Holy Spirit now will do *in* us. In the declaration of verse 9, "You, however, are not in the realm of the flesh but are in the realm of the Spirit, if indeed the Spirit of God lives in you," God makes good on the promise he gave Ezekiel (36:27) "And I will put my Spirit in you and move you to follow my decrees and be careful to keep my laws."

Because of our inability, God took two steps to deal with our problem. First, he sent his Son in the flesh, who died for sin and in doing so condemned sin in the flesh. Then, God also sent the Holy Spirit to dwell inside us that we may "walk … in the Spirit."

It's a walk; not a work. We depend "according to His power, which mightily works within me" (Colossians 1:29). That's why Paul contrasts the works of the flesh with the fruit of the Spirit. (Galatians 5:19, 22) Not our effort but the work of the Spirit in us produces the fruit.

To "walk after" is subjective. Walking after the flesh I yield to the dictates of the flesh, which brings me into conflict with God. But walking after the Spirit brings me into subjection to the Spirit. If I'm walking after the Spirit, I can't be independent of him. I must be subject to the Holy Spirit. The initiative must be with him.

Only when I yield do I find the law of the spirit of life being fulfilled—not by me but in me. "For all who are being led by the Spirit of God, these are sons of God" (Romans 8:14 NASB).

Being a son of God is important. In a sense we become children of God when we're saved, however we aren't living in that legacy until we're filled with and led by the Holy Spirit. Otherwise it's as if we've invited a guest into our house, but we close all the interior doors because we don't want our guest to see how we really live.

When we asked the Lord to forgive our sins and enter our lives, our heart became the residence of a living person: the third person of the Trinity. The Holy Spirit opens the Scriptures to our understanding, directs our prayers, governs our lives, and reproduces the character of Jesus in us. But for the Holy Spirit to accomplish all that (and more) we have to surrender to his leadership. We have to open the doors.

We are now ready, perhaps, to talk about why God did all this. It can be summarized to two phrases, drawn of the earlier and the latter sections of Romans. God's purpose in both creation and redemption was "the glory of God" (Romans 3:23), but also "that the creation itself also will be set free from its slavery to corruption into the freedom of the glory of the children of God" (Romans 8:21 NASB). God's goal is to restore us and all of creation to the glory he originally planned.

Here we are, eating mud pies when he has spread a banquet for us.

"What distinguishes the children of God?" Andrew Murray asks. "It is that God dwells in the midst of them and reveals Himself to them in power."

> Then the LORD said: "I am making a covenant with you. Before all your people I will do wonders never before done in any nation in all the world. The people you live among will see how awesome is the work that I, the LORD, will do for you." (Exodus 34:10)

Seen any wonders recently?

Sin thwarted God's purpose for us by causing us to miss God's glory. Remember that "all have sinned and fall short of the glory of God"? (Romans 3:23). When we think of sin, we usually think of judgment. We think of punishment, but God thinks of all the good, the power, the glory we're missing.

Because of sin we forfeit God's glory; because of redemption we are qualified once again for that glory. God's great, eternal plan has always been glory. Glory for the creation, glory for the creature, glory of God.

So, this consideration moves us on.

> The Spirit Himself testifies with our spirit that we are children of God, and if children, heirs also, heirs of God and fellow heirs with Christ, if indeed we suffer with Him so that we may also be glorified with Him. For I consider that the sufferings of this present time are not worthy to be compared with the glory that is to be revealed to us. (Romans 8:16-18 NASB)

> For those whom He foreknew, He also predestined to become conformed to the image of His Son, so that He would be the firstborn among many brethren; and these whom He predestined, He also called; and these whom He called, He also justified; and these whom He justified, He also glorified. (8:29-30 NASB)

What is God's objective? That his son Jesus Christ should be the firstborn among many brothers and sisters.

In John 1:14, we are told "The Word became flesh and made his dwelling among us. We have seen his glory, the glory of the One and Only, who came from the Father." God had no other son but this one. How then does the only begotten son becomes the first begotten son? Simple: by the Father having more children. How does that happen? Through first the creation, then the redemption of the world. He wants us; he'll not be satisfied without us.

"For the creation waits in eager expectation for the children of God to be revealed" (Romans 8:19). God planned all this from the beginning. Our being children of God is not an add-on to the plan; it *is* the plan.

Read again about the prodigal son in Luke 15. We usually see the point of view of the younger son, but Jesus also tells us something about the father. The point of the parable isn't about the bad time the son experienced, but about his salvation. The climax of the first part is the father's exultation, "For this son of mine was dead and is alive again; he was lost and is found" (Luke 15:24). Jesus is describing how much God the Father loves and seeks us.

Jesus was the only begotten son. No spiritual brothers. But God's purpose in the creation and the redemption was, "bringing many sons to glory" (Hebrews 2:10). In Romans 8:29 we read of "many brothers", and in Hebrews of "many sons." From Jesus' point of view, we're brothers; from Father's, we're sons.

God wants lots of full-grown, mature sons. Not living in the fields or pig sties; he wants them home, to share his glory. As he explains in Romans 8:30 (NASB), "these whom He justified, He also glorified." How does he bring this about? By justifying, then glorifying us.

Jesus explains how the only begotten son becomes the first begotten son in John 12:24. "I tell you the truth, unless a kernel of wheat falls to the ground and dies, it remains only a single seed. But if it dies, it produces many seeds." Who is the kernel? Jesus. In the whole universe God had but one grain of wheat; one begotten son.

Whom he loved. That grain was planted in the ground: dead. But Jesus did not stay in the grave. And from the resurrection—the sprouting of that one grain of wheat sprang many grains. We are the fruit; we are the new seed. The multiplication continues today.

So we who are born of the spirit "become partakers of the divine nature" (2 Peter 1:4 NASB). Not by our own merits, but by virtue of our being "in Christ." "For you haven't received a spirit of slavery leading to fear again, but you've received a spirit of adoption as sons by which we cry out, "Abba! Father!" The Spirit Himself testifies with our spirit that we are children of God" (Romans 8:15-16 NASB).

We're God's children. Not slaves, not servants, not clients, but children. By the obedience of his only begotten son, the Father has secured many sons and daughters.

Notice how John records the transition. John 1:12 reports that Jesus came into the world that "all who received him, to those who believed in his name, he gave the right to become children of God." Then in John 20:17, Jesus says to Mary Magdalene, "Go instead to my brothers and tell them, 'I am returning to my Father and your Father, to my God and your God.'"

Do you get it? Before, Jesus spoke of "the Father" and "my Father." After the resurrection, he says, "your Father." It's a done deal. He calls us "my brothers." As Hebrews 2:11 records, "So Jesus is not ashamed to call them brothers."

Praise God, we're in. Not by anything we did or could ever do, but by what Jesus accomplished 2,000 years ago.

Back to Genesis. In the midst of the garden of Eden, God planted two trees: the tree of life and the tree of the knowledge of good and evil. Adam was created innocent; he had no knowledge of good and evil. Think of a grown man—whether thirty years old or maybe a hundred—with no sense of right or wrong. Undeveloped much?

> The Lord God took the man and put him in the Garden of Eden to work it and take care of it. And the Lord God commanded the man, "You are free to eat from any tree in the garden; but you must not eat from the tree of the knowledge of good and evil, for when you eat from it you will certainly die." (Genesis 2:15-17)

The knowledge of good and evil in itself is not wrong. In fact, without it Adam can't decide moral issues for himself. He has to depend on … God. You see, there are two ways to live life. Depending on God, or depending on yourself.

You know what happened. Instead of depending on God, Adam disobeyed. Remember Satan's exact point of temptation was "your eyes will be opened, and you will be like God, knowing good and evil" (Genesis 3:5). Satan didn't lie that time. Sometimes half-truths can be more misleading than outright lies. As a self-sufficient creature, Adam would possess the power of independent judgment.

Adam chose to eat of the tree of the knowledge of good and evil. In doing so he became a fully-developed man. For the fruit was "also desirable for gaining wisdom" (Genesis 3:6), but the consequence was death because his choice involved disobeying God (not to mention his complicity with Satan).

Adam could live a divine life depending on God or a human life independent of God. Adam chose independence. What is your choice?

We've been doing the same ever since. Even when we choose to do good, we do it because it's right in our eyes, not out of obedience to God.

I'm being too hard, you say? How many of us explain the commandments and laws of the Old Testament in terms of natural survival? How many of us excuse ourselves from following Jesus' New Testament commandments with legalistic hair-splitting? We're just like Adam and Eve, wanting to be like God. To judge for ourselves. So, we like Adam are subject to the law of sin and doomed to die. Then Jesus came as the last Adam.

In the same sense that we were in the first Adam when he sinned, we were in Jesus when he died.

There's more. Jesus rose and (1 Corinthians 15:45) "The last Adam became a life-giving spirit." Now each of us can receive him and partake in the resurrection life.

> Yet to all who did receive him, to those
> who believed in his name, he gave the right
> to become children of God—even to those

> who believe in His name, children born not
> of natural descent, nor of human decision
> or a husband's will, but born of God. (John
> 1:12-13)

God isn't out to reform your life. He doesn't want you as you are. He can't—or won't—bring the natural man to glory. It's like trying to make your dog a member of your family. He may be a very good dog, but he's a dog, not a human. The same applies to your relationship with God. As long as you are a natural man or woman, you can't belong to the divine family. You must become a new man, born of God. Justification and regeneration go together.

We can possess more than Adam lost. Adam, at best, was just a under-developed man. We can possess the life that Adam missed, because we're born in a way he never was.

For this reason—and only this—we can live a life of holiness. It isn't just our lives which have been changed, but the life of God has been transplanted—imparted to us.

The whole question of sin becomes out of place. Sin came in with Adam. Even when it's dealt with, we're only back to where Adam was. But, in pursuit of the divine purpose, Jesus redeemed us, giving us far more than Adam ever had. He made us partakers in the very life of God.

How? Through the presence and the ministry of the Holy Spirit. "God has poured out his love into our hearts by the Holy Spirit, whom he has given us" (Romans 5:5).

Or, stated negatively as Paul did in Romans 8:9 (NASB), "But if anyone does not have the Spirit of Christ, he does not belong to Him." God's gifts are free, but they're given with a purpose. He has "blessed us in the heavenly realms with every spiritual blessing in Christ" (Ephesians 1:3).

If these blessing are to become ours in practice (as opposed to just in revelation), we must appropriate them.

Study Questions

Chapter 9
Spirit Poured Out

1. Read Romans Chapter 8. Seriously, read it straight through. Right now. Isn't that great news?
2. Are you experiencing life and peace? Are you walking in the spirit? How does the Spirit's presence work and change your very nature?
3. Do you participate in the glory of God? Are you a child of God?
4. Why is hope so important to a believer?
5. What do you need to change to surrender control of your life to God's spirit? Not what you do for God, but what you let God do for you?

CHAPTER 10

SPIRIT IN-DWELLING

Romans 8

◆

THE HOLY SPIRIT is given to us in two ways: outpoured and indwelling. The distinction is significant because we're often happy to have it poured upon us but less cooperative to have it dwelling within us.

Peter explained Pentecost to the crowd which had gathered when they heard the sound of the spirit-filled disciples speaking in tongues (Acts 2:4). After pointing out this was the pouring out of God's Spirit spoken of by the prophet Joel (Acts 2:16), Peter declared of Jesus, "Exalted to the right hand of God, he has received from the Father the promised Holy Spirit and has poured out what you now see and hear" (Acts 2:33). And that "God has made this Jesus, whom you crucified, both Lord and Christ" (Acts 2:36).

The pouring out of the Holy Spirit has no relation to your merits or mine, but to Jesus'. He is glorified; the Spirit is poured out.

Peter declared that the outpouring of the Spirit proves the Lordship of Jesus Christ. How do we know that Jesus is Lord and Christ? Because he pours out his Spirit on us, then and now. If the gift of the Spirit depends on who Jesus is, is it possible that the Jesus has been glorified and you have somehow not received the Spirit? No. On the same ground as your sins being forgiven on the shedding of Jesus' blood. The blood has been shed; you are redeemed. The Lord has been glorified, therefore the Spirit has been poured out on you. Yes, you.

Wait, you say, I may agree with that in my mind, but I haven't experienced it. Am I supposed to sit here and say I have everything when I know perfectly well that I have nothing? I can't work miracles. I don't speak in tongues. My prayers don't move mountains. So? Just because you haven't experienced one particular of God's truth doesn't invalidate the whole of it. The truth rests on the objective facts. We desire the subjective experience, but our experience also rests on the facts. Remember knowing and reckoning? God's facts are the basis for our experience.

Perhaps the problem is that, while the Spirit has been poured out on you, the Spirit doesn't presently fill you (Ephesians 5:18). A. W. Tozer suggests four essential steps to being filled with the Holy Spirit.

First, presenting your body as a vessel to receive the Holy Spirit.

> Therefore I urge you, brethren, by the
> mercies of God, to present your bodies a
> living and holy sacrifice, acceptable to God,
> which is your spiritual service of worship.
> And do not be conformed to this world,
> but be transformed by the renewing of your
> mind. (Romans 12:1-2 NASB)

Second, asking to receive the Holy Spirit. "If you then, though you are evil, know how to give good gifts to your children, how much more will your Father in heaven give the Holy Spirit to those who ask him!" (Luke 11:11-12).

Third, obeying God. "We are witnesses of these things, and so is the Holy Spirit, whom God has given to those who obey him" (Acts 5:32). How many of us whine about not receiving the Spirit while we disobey his commands? Obedience is not just a good idea; it's fundamental.

Fourth, believing you will receive it. "I would like to learn just one thing from you: Did you receive the Spirit by the works of the law, or by believing what you heard?" (Galatians 3:2).

Tozer continues, "Every Christian has a measure of the Holy Spirit and do not let anyone argue you out of that. 'If anyone does not have the Spirit of Christ, they do not belong to Christ.' (Romans 8:9), and so He has given us a deposit of the Holy Spirit." But, "our problem is that we do not want to go through the experience of being filling with the Spirit. We want to be blessed, to go to heaven, to wear a crown, and rule five cities."

You can pray and wait for years and never experience the Spirit's power, because you haven't presented yourself, asked, obeyed or believed. The block is not on God's end, but on yours.

When you cease to plead and bargain, but begin instead accepting God at his word and praising (not to mention presenting, asking, obeying and believing) him, perhaps your problem is solved. Not that you will immediately receive any particular manifestation of the Spirit's presence but that you will no longer require it.

Jesus isn't going to be made Lord; he is Lord. Therefore, I'm not going to receive the Holy Spirit; I have received it. Now I'm filled with it. It's a faith that comes by revelation.

Peter goes on at Pentecost, saying:

> Repent, and each of you be baptized in the name of Jesus Christ for the forgiveness of your sins; and you will receive the gift of the Holy Spirit. For the promise is for you and your children and for all who are far off, as many as the Lord our God will call to Himself. (Acts 2:38-39 NASB)

Do you hear that? All. What part of all doesn't include you? Wait, you say, that only happened at Pentecost. Really? Peter said, "and for all who are far off." Aren't we among those "far off"?

Consider this example from your own experience: you've read Scripture, perhaps all of your life. Perhaps over and over. You thought about it, read commentaries on it, perhaps even prayed about it. You thought you understood what God was saying. But suddenly, a particular passage jumps out at you. Wow! You hadn't seen *that* before. Suddenly you understand it. It's the Spirit himself testifying to your spirit. (Romans 8:15) Not just of your being a child of God, but also of all spiritual truth.

Paul confirms (1 Corinthians 2:14) "The man without the Spirit does not accept the things that come from the Spirit of God, for they are foolishness to him, and he cannot understand them, because they are spiritually discerned." John wrote, "You have an anointing from the Holy One, and all of you know the truth" (1 John 2:20).

Tozer, Nee, Joyner, Meyers and Frangipane are smart, spirit-filled people, but they aren't the source of your revelation. It's not even Luke or Paul. It's the Holy Spirit.

Has that happened to you? If so, then you understand. The outpoured Holy Spirit is more than theoretical. It's part of your history. If not, you *will* understand someday. In the meantime maybe it's you—your old sin nature—which blocks you from experiencing the gifts and works of the Spirit.

The point is that Spirit has been poured out on us, whether we experience it or not—and we may not. But whether or not we experience glorious manifestations of the poured out Spirit, God's goal is to lead us to the indwelling of the Holy Spirit, fulfilling the promise he made to Ezekiel (36:27), "I will put my Spirit in you."

Paul writes to the Romans, "… if indeed the Spirit of God lives in you" (8:9 NASB). "And if the Spirit of Him who raised Jesus from the dead dwells in you …" (Romans 8:11 NASB). As with the outpoured Spirit, if we are to experience that fact, first we need a divine revelation.

Watchman Nee tells us, "When we see Jesus as Lord objectively—as exalted in heaven—then we will experience the outpouring of the Holy Spirit upon us. When we see Jesus as Lord subjectively—as effective ruler of our lives—then we will know the power of the Spirit within us."

Remember how the Corinthians were so preoccupied with the visible signs of the Holy Spirit's outpouring—making much of tongues and miracles—while at the same time their lives were full of contradictions and Paul reproached them in Jesus' name? (1 Corinthians 12 & 14). They'd obviously received the Spirit, but they were spiritually immature. "Fireworks" Christians, A. W. Tozer would call them.

The remedy then is the same remedy we need today.

Paul writes (1 Cor 3:16), "Don't you know that you yourselves are God's temple and that God's Spirit lives in you?"

We must understand: to have the Spirit is to have God living in us. Many of us consider the Holy Spirit to be a mere influence, like our consciences. Paul reminds us just who dwells in our hearts: God. We are earthen vessels but we carry a treasure of unspeakable worth: the Lord of Glory. You, who have been born again, carry God in your heart. The creator of the universe came into your heart and made it—what? His shack? His mansion? No, His temple.

The reason many Christians don't experience the power of the Spirit is because they lack reverence. You aren't just standing on holy ground, you *are* holy ground.

Wherever you go, whatever you do, the God of the universe is with you. Is with you now. It's a fact, but many Christians don't see it. If you were truly aware of the Spirit's indwelling, it would transform your life. The problem is that too many of us haven't surrendered—haven't given way in our souls for the Holy Spirit to connect with and guide our spirit. We haven't followed Tozer's four steps.

Paul continues, "Do you not know that your body is a temple of the Holy Spirit, who is in you, whom you have received from God? You are not your own; you were bought at a price. Therefore honor God with your body" (1 Cor 6:19-20).

You aren't your own. Full surrender should follow. Consecration should follow revelation. The difference between victorious and defeated Christians is that the former recognize the divine ownership of their lives; the others live as if they were their own masters.

A day must come, as definite as the day we were saved, when we give up ourselves and submit to the absolute lordship of Jesus Christ. When we surrender everything to him. From that day we're no longer our own masters, but only stewards.

If we don't give him absolute authority, he'll be present (poured out) but he can't be powerful (in dwelling). Because we keep getting in his way.

See how God works with us in Paul's benediction in 2 Corinthians 13:14: "May the grace of the Lord Jesus Christ, and the love of God, and the fellowship of the Holy Spirit be with you all." The love of God is the source of all spiritual blessing; the grace of Jesus made all that spiritual wealth available to us; and the communion of the Holy Spirit remains to impart it to us. What the father devised, the son accomplished, and the spirit communicates to us. That's why the Holy Spirit came— to make real in us all that is ours through the finished work of Jesus Christ.

Are you living for the Lord or yourself? Is there anything he's asking of you that you're withholding? Our complete surrender often hinges on one thing—maybe even a good thing—but he must have our all. Psalm 73:25 says, "Whom have I in heaven but you? And earth has nothing I desire besides you." Can you truly say, "There is nothing on earth I desire besides you"?

If we yield everything to him, we don't need to wait for special feelings or supernatural manifestations, but simply to look up and praise him for what has already happened. Thank him that the glory of God has already filled his temple—your body.

The eighth chapter of Romans contains Paul's core argument: Jesus' death and resurrection purchased our redemption, which leads us back to God's original purpose for mankind. We weren't just designed to have the Spirit poured out on us, but for it to dwell in us. The Spirit doesn't dwell in us until we substantiate it in faith.

"The mind governed by the flesh is death, but the mind governed by the Spirit is life and peace" (Romans 8:6).

What does being governed by the indwelling Spirit mean? And how does that differ from our conceptions, which are often based on the external manifestations of the Spirit's out pouring? The Holy Spirit is one, as God is one, but we see it working in different ways, and we may mistake *some* of its actions for *all* its of actions.

Paul declares, "Those who are led by the Spirit of God are sons of God" (Romans 8:14).

> For those whom He foreknew, He also predestined to become conformed to the image of His Son, so that He would be the firstborn among many brethren; and these whom He predestined, He also called; and these whom He called, He also justified; and these whom He justified, He also glorified. (Romans 8:29-30 NASB)

Here is Paul's climax. Not only does God know, destine, call, choose and prepare us to become his children, but he also makes us like Jesus in his glory. Paul then asks

(Romans 8:31 NASB), "What then shall we say to these things? If God is for us, who is against us?" What's left to say? "Will He not also with Him freely give us all things? (Romans 8:32 NASB).

Justification leads to glorification, but not just the glory of one, but the glorification of all who manifest the image of the One.

> In all these things we overwhelmingly conquer through Him who loved us. For I am convinced that neither death, nor life, nor angels, nor principalities, nor things present, nor things to come, nor powers, nor height, nor depth, nor any other created thing, will be able to separate us from the love of God, which is in Christ Jesus our Lord. (Romans 8:37-39 NASB)

Paul says, if we don't have the Holy Spirit, we have nothing. But we do have it—each one of you who accepted Jesus as your savior.

But we aren't *living* in the Spirit. We are quick to claim the victory in the verses above while ignoring everything Paul tells us in chapters 5, 6 and 7. Context is important, especially in the Bible. And when those promised victories don't happen—or happen spasmodically—we blame God. No, God did/does/will do his part. It's we who aren't doing ours. Or do it sporadically.

Now that the Spirit is dwelling in us our "low fuel" light is finally extinguished. Our sins are washed away by his Blood, our sin nature has been killed by the Cross, the Spirit of God has been poured out on us and dwells in us. What more could God possible have for us?

Lots more.

Study Questions

Chapter 10
Spirit In-dwelling

1. Have you repented and been baptized?

2. Has the Holy Spirit been poured out on you?

3. Is Jesus your lord? Objectively (as exalted in heaven)? Subjectively (as effective ruler of your life)?

4. Do you know that you are God's temple and that his spirit lives in you? Are you holy ground? Do you experience his indwelling? Have you surrendered everything to him?

5. Are you living for God or for yourself? Are you withholding something from him?

6. How strong is God's love for you? What needs can God's love meet in your life?

7. Practically speaking, how can the Spirit empower you for victory over sin today?

8. What do you need to change in your life so that the Spirit dwells in you?

CHAPTER 11

OTHERS

Romans 9 and 10

◆

THE EIGHTH CHAPTER of Romans contains the first half of Paul's core message. Before he concludes it in chapter 12, Paul makes a three chapter digression into God's sovereign dealings with the Jewish people. Why?

Perhaps he or the Holy Spirit knew that right about here we're getting cocky. We're thinking, "Look at me. I'm special. God chose me." Well, he did choose you, but that doesn't make you the chosen people.

The Jews are the chosen people. But remember, God chose them, not vice versa. Not because they were smart or powerful or good. Abram wasn't even looking for a new god to follow when God first called him. (see Genesis 12) God called him.

Romans 9, 10 and 11 develop the themes Paul expounded in the first eight chapters as well as information relevant to how we should live relative to the unsaved.

Make no mistake, the Jews are still the chosen people. It is about the Jewish people that Paus writes, "God's gifts and his call are irrevocable" (Romans 11:29). Paul wants Israel saved. He is a Jew himself. He wants his fellow Jews saved so badly that he offers himself to be cut off from the kingdom of God for the sake of his fellow Jews. (Romans 9:3) But he also notes that their failure to accept salvation is not due to the failure of God's Word. (Romans 9:6)

Then Paul discusses who is and who is not a child of Abraham. This distinction stems from God's blessing resting on the child of the covenant, Isaac, and not the child of Sarah's maid, Ishmael. Before we follow Paul's discussion of God's sovereignty, let's pause and consider what being the children of the promise implies today.

From the Jewish point of view, all humanity is divided into the Jew and the non-Jew (or *goyim*, in Hebrew, literally, "the nations"). Christians, Moslems, Hindus, Buddhists, atheists are all the same to them. If anything, Christians and Moslems may be worse than Hindus and Buddhists because, from the Jewish point of view, we have twisted the Hebrew faith into something that looks false and diabolical.

Like the Jews, most Christians have a two-way division of humankind ("us and them"), but Paul's first letter to the Corinthians (10:32) suggests three categories: "Give offense to none, neither to the Jews, nor to Gentiles, nor to the Church of God." God, of course, is no respecter of persons (Acts 10:34)—He loves all of us. However, not everyone has accepted God's offer of redemption.

God wants none to perish and has a plan for all, starting—and ending—with the Jews.

> The LORD had said to Abram, "Go from your country, your people and your father's household to the land I will show you. I will make you into a great nation, and I will bless you; I will make your name great, and you will be a blessing. I will bless those who bless you, and whoever curses you I will curse; and all peoples on earth will be blessed through you." (Genesis 12:1-3)

Later God clarifies, "It is through Isaac that your offspring will be reckoned" (Genesis 21:12). God separated a people unto himself: the Jews.

Until Jesus came, the Jews were partakers of God's covenant, while the Gentiles were "excluded from citizenship in Israel and foreigners to the covenants of the promise, without hope and without God" (Ephesians 2:12).

On the cross, God took away the partition, allowing all who believed to become the body of Jesus Christ, as we studied previously. So those believers who had been Jews and had been Gentiles became the body of Christ: the Church—the third category, within which there are neither Greek nor Jew. (Romans 10:12)

Just as the Old Testament prophets decried the Jews who rejected God then, some later Jews did not accept Jesus as their Messiah and savior. Not because God's word failed, but because of their hearts were hard. So, Paul hoped that his ministry to the Gentiles would stir the Jews to jealousy and maybe to reconsider the grace of God and believe Jesus.

Paul repeats the quote from Genesis to emphasize that "it is not the children of the flesh who are children of God, but the children of the promise are regarded as descendants" (Romans 9:8 NASB).

Twice God separated Abraham's natural offspring to identify the chosen people. First, choosing Isaac over Ishmael, (Gen 21:10) "Get rid of that slave woman and her son, for that woman's son will never share in the inheritance with my son Isaac." Then choosing Jacob over Esau. Paul quotes Malachi (1:3), "Jacob I loved, but Esau I hated." These two elections focused God's promise on a particular people: the descendants of Jacob, whose name was changed to "Israel." (Genesis 32:28 and 35:10)

Paul justifies this selection on the basis of God's sovereignty. There can be no doubt that some are picked and some are not. (Romans 9:16) It does not, therefore, depend on human desire or effort, but on God's mercy. Using the example of Pharaoh, Paul continues, "So then He has mercy on whom He desires, and He hardens whom He desires" (Romans 9:18 NASB).

This is a hard teaching. It seems at odds with the idea that God loves everyone and offers salvation to all without respect. And I have no easy answer to that issue.

Now Paul's imaginary heckler pipes up to point out that he is therefore not to blame for his doom because no one can resist the will of God. Paul replies that makes as much sense as the pot complaining about how it was fashioned (Romans 9:19-20).

Next Paul suggests what God had in mind all this time. "He did so to make known the riches of His glory upon vessels of mercy, which He prepared beforehand for glory, even us, whom He also called, not from among Jews only, but also from among Gentiles?" (Romans 9:23-24 NASB).

What if the Jews' apparent rejection of Jesus was part of God's plan to woo the other objects of his mercy? So that, as he says in Hosea: "I will call them 'my people' who are not my people; and I will call her 'my loved one' who is not my loved one," and, "In the very place where it was said to them, 'You are not my people,' there they will be called 'children of the living God'" (Romans 9:25-26).

Why, you ask? "That the Gentiles, who did not pursue righteousness, have obtained it, a righteousness that is by faith; but the people of Israel, who pursued the law as the way of righteousness, have not attained their goal. Why not? Because they pursued it not by faith but as if it were by works" (Romans 9:30-32).

Perhaps some of us who call ourselves Christians are in the same state as the people of Israel: saying we belong to God, but seeking to please him by our works, not by that spiritual connection that makes us alive in Christ: the very thing Paul just addressed in Romans 8. But God, much less Paul, hasn't given up on Israel.

"For I can testify about them that they have a zeal for God, but not in accordance with knowledge" (Romans 10:2 NASB). They think they know what they're doing, but they don't. Since they pursued their salvation by works, they could not die to sin nor to their sin nature. In rejecting Christ, they rejected God and missed his righteousness.

Oh, they tried to follow the law.

As Moses said, "The person who does these things will live by them" (Leviticus 18:5, Romans 10:5). But it is the righteousness based on faith, which can say "The word is near you; it is in your mouth and in your heart" (Deuteronomy 30:14, Romans 10:8). Aren't many of us in that same boat?

Here Paul inserts his great formula for becoming a Christian: "If you confess with your mouth Jesus as Lord, and believe in your heart that God raised Him from the dead, you will be saved" (Romans 10:9 NASB).

It's as simple as that. Publicly confess him as your lord—meaning your lord and master, whom you will obey—and believe in the resurrection. Faith is not making yourself believe what is not true. The natural is true, but there's truth beyond the natural. Because, as Paul quotes Isaiah (Isaiah 28:16, Romans 10:11 NASB), "Whoever believes in him will not be disappointed." Paul continues,

"For there is no distinction between Jew and Greek; for the same Lord is Lord of all, abounding in riches for all who call on Him; for, 'Whoever will call on the name of the Lord will be saved'" (Joel 3:32, Romans 10:13 NASB). Did you hear that? Do you believe that? "'Whoever will call on the name of the Lord will be saved.'"

Whoever.

Anyone.

You.

I must point out that that verse apparently contradicts the words of Jesus. In the parable of the ten virgins, Jesus says to those who called him "Lord," "I never knew you" (Matthew 25:11-12).

The reconciliation is simple. Listen closely.

When we say the Lord Jesus Christ, we say a lot and mean even more. Jesus was the earthly name of the man who was the son of God. "Christ" is the Greek word translating the Hebrew "Messiah." Both words mean, "anointed." So by calling Jesus the Messiah, we are recognizing him as God's special envoy to bring us back to God. Jesus often referred to himself as "Son of Man" in the same sense. (Daniel referred to the "Son of Man" or "like a son of man" in his prophetic writings.) Finally, comes the word "lord," which in both the Hebrew and the Greek refers to one we recognize as our master.

None of these words—even taken together—approach the concept of God or Son of God. That is something you have to settle in your heart. You must. Failing to decide is, itself, a decision. This is the core of Paul's message. What you believe in your heart makes all the difference, just as Paul warns us (Romans 10:9).

Do you believe that Jesus the man—the anointed one of God—whom we call our master—was and is and will be, in fact, God? Equal with—in fact, inseparable from—God the Father and God the Holy Spirit? If you repeat Paul's salvation formula, you proclaim Jesus as lord of your life, and if you believe in your heart—that is, at the core of your being—that God raised him from the dead, then you are confessing that the man who lived in Galilee two thousand years ago existed before the creation of time and space and that he will someday come to gather his brothers and sisters to live with him forever.

Salvation is not just a matter of words, but of the transformation of our hearts.

Is that kind of proclamation too big a leap for you? Then start where you are. Proclaim and believe and act as if Jesus is your lord and master in the narrower sense. Follow him—his teachings and his example—daily. Obey him. That's quite a bit for most of us. If we call him "lord," it should transform our behavior. Jesus asked "Why do you call me, 'Lord, Lord,' and do not do what I say?" (Luke 6:40). Smith Wigglesworth promises, as you experience him your faith will grow.

Just before he spoke "Not everyone who says to me, 'Lord, Lord,' will enter the kingdom of heaven, but only the one who does the will of my Father who is in heaven," (Matthew 7:21) Jesus proclaimed, "You will know them by their fruits" (Matthew 7:20 NASB). This is one of the hardest teachings of Jesus. He proclaims time and again that there will be people who say they are believers—who believe they are saved—but who will be left outside the gates of the New Jerusalem. Not where I want to spend eternity.

What is your guarantee against that? The second half of Paul's formula. Believing in your heart that God raised him from the dead.

Don't be fooled into thinking that accepting Jesus is a matter of glib words. Merely mouthing the formula doesn't assure you all the benefits of salvation here and now, let alone eternity in heaven. John MacArthur said, "The object of faith, however, is not a divine offer, but the person of Jesus Christ. Faith in Him is what saves, not just believing His promises or accepting facts about Him. Saving faith has to be more than accepting facts. Even demons have that (accepting facts) kind of faith (see James 2:19)."

This is not a mental exercise. Not a word game. What's in your heart?

Salvation isn't just a promise, but the fulfillment of God's promises. It loops us all the way back to the opening of Romans, where Paul declared, "For in the gospel the righteousness of God is revealed—a righteousness that is by faith from first to last, just as it is written: 'The righteous will live by faith'" (Romans 1:17). To what end?

Martin Luther wrote, "Faith is a work of God in us, which changes us and brings us to birth anew from God. It kills the old Adam and makes us completely different people in heart, mind, senses, and all our powers, and brings the Holy Spirit with it." There is no other way to be saved.

The ones rejected in the Matthew 25 parable were those whose actions did not match their supposed faith. As we have already quoted James (2:14 NASB), "What use is it, my brethren, if someone says he has faith but he has no works? Can that faith save him?" Their faith should have produced works of love. Notice, those who produced works of love did so without seeking recognition or reward, or even knowing they were serving Jesus when they served their fellows.

Having gotten our relationship with God on that solid ground, Paul now relates it to the lost of Israel—and all who are unsaved.

"How then will they call on Him in whom they have not believed? How will they believe in Him whom they have not heard? And how will they hear without a preacher?" (Romans 10:14 NASB). He admits that "not all the Israelites accepted the good news" (Romans 10:16).

Oh, they heard it. Do you remember how, as recorded in Acts, on his missionary journeys every time Paul entered a new city in what is now Turkey and Greece he first went to the local synagogue to bring the good news of Christ to his fellow Jews before he shared it with the Gentiles? But uniformly, they rejected him.

The only exception were the Jews in Berea (Acts 17:10-13). After Paul and Silas were almost killed by a mob in Thessalonica, the Jews in Berea "received the message with great eagerness and examined the Scriptures every day to see if what Paul said was true." That's how we should receive the good news.

So, the Jews heard the message. "Their voice has gone out into all the earth, and their words to the ends of the world" (Romans 10:18 NASB, Psalm 19:4). And they understood it. Paul quotes, "Moses says, 'I will make you jealous by that which is not a nation, by a nation without understanding will I anger you'" (Romans 10:19 NASB, Deuteronomy 32:21). Then Isaiah "I was found by those who did not seek Me, I became manifest to those who did not ask for me." Finally declaring, "All day long I have stretched out My hands to a disobedient and obstinate people" (Romans 10:20-21 NASB, Isaiah 65:1-2).

Harsh. But words of hope also. All day long God holds out his hands to his chosen people.

And to you.

Study Questions

Chapter 11
Others

1. How do you feel about the Jews being the people of the covenant? Does the rejection of Jesus by some Jews, then or now, justify the Holocaust? Does it nullify their status as the chosen people?

2. Is God obligated to save anyone? Why or why not? Why do the doctrines of divine sovereignty and election make many people uncomfortable or downright angry?

3. Do you ever feel that God is unfair? In what circumstances?

4. What comfort do you find knowing that God is in control instead of trusting in chance or fate?

5. When you say, "Jesus is Lord," what do you mean? Do you mean a good man who lived and died 2000 years ago? Or do you mean God? Is he your master or just a mentor, friend, or casual acquaintance? What do you believe in the core of your being? What would you be willing to die— or live—for?

6. If you don't believe, do you at least know that God still waits for you with open arms?

CHAPTER 12

God's Plan

Romans 11

◆

If the Jews continue to be "a disobedient and obstinate people," (Romans 10:21 NASB) "I ask then: Did God reject his people? By no means!" (11:1). Paul reminds us that he is a Jew himself. To Elijah, afraid he was the sole surviving prophet, God responded that he had reserved seven thousand who had not bowed to Baal. "So too, at the present time there is a remnant chosen by grace" (Romans 11:5).

Paul then cites several Old Testament sources implying that God actively dulled the receptivity of his chosen people, that the whole world might be saved.

What so many Jews and Christians fail to achieve by works, some achieve by grace. And those who don't? "Did they stumble so as to fall beyond recovery? Not at all!

Rather, because of their transgression, salvation has come to the Gentiles to make Israel envious" (Romans 11:11).

Now Paul addresses the Gentiles:

> I take pride in my ministry in the hope that I may somehow arouse my own people to envy and save some of them. For if their rejection brought reconciliation to the world, what will their acceptance be but life from the dead? (Romans 11:13-15)

You know the metaphor of grafted in branches. Jesus used it in John 15 to describe how we were grafted into the kingdom. Paul uses it again here.

> But if some of the branches were broken off, and you, being a wild olive, were grafted in among them and became partaker with them of the rich root of the olive tree, do not be arrogant toward the branches; but if you are arrogant, remember that it is not you who supports the root, but the root supports you. You will say then, "Branches were broken off so that I might be grafted in." Quite right, they were broken off for their unbelief, but you stand by your faith. Do not be conceited, but fear; for if God did not spare the natural branches, He will not spare you, either. (Romans 11:17-21 NASB)

Note that last warning: if God didn't spare the people of the covenant because of their unbelief and disobedience, he won't spare us.

But those who do believe may be restored. "If they do not continue in their unbelief, will be grafted in, for God is able to graft them in again" (Romans 11:23 NASB).

Then Paul lets us in on a secret, least we become conceited in our new position of grace: "a partial hardening has happened to Israel until the fullness of the Gentiles has come in; and so all Israel will be saved" (Romans 11:25-26 NASB).

What's that all about? Partial? Some will believe, and some won't. God has allowed the Jews not to see his truth for a season. How does that come about?

In 2 Corinthians 3:15, Paul writes, "even today when they read Moses' writings, their hearts are covered with that veil, and they do not understand." Their hearts are blinded. Until when? "Until the full number of the Gentiles has come in." Is Paul saying that God is intentionally allowing most Jews to remain outside the kingdom out of mercy for the unsaved Gentiles? Apparently.

When he cries over the city on Palm Sunday, Jesus says:

> "Jerusalem, Jerusalem, you who kill the prophets and stone those sent to you, how often I have longed to gather your children together, as a hen gathers her chicks under her wings, and you were not willing. Look, your house is left to you desolate. For I tell you, you will not see me again until you say,

'Blessed is he who comes in the name of the
Lord.'" (Matthew 23:39)

Not until they recognize Jesus as their Messiah and praise him. Bless him. God has not forgotten the Jews. The new covenant, after all, was originally offered to them. So, to rip the scales from their eyes, God plans to move mightily among the Gentiles—the unsaved Gentiles.

Lest there be any doubt, Paul asserts "For God has shut up all in disobedience so that He may show mercy to all" (Romans 11:32 NASB). All, as in everyone.

So, what is "the full number of the Gentiles?" Who were this people who were no people; this nation who were "not a nation"? The Gentiles, of course. Not just you and me, but all the unsaved who weren't Jews.

Remember the three way division of mankind? Jews, Gentiles, the Church.

The world's current population is about seven billion, of whom slightly over 2 billion identify themselves as Christians and 14 to 18 million are Jews. Therefore, close to 5 billion are unsaved "Gentiles." Yet we complacently sit back and say, "Well, almost everyone who's going to be saved has been saved. It's time for Jesus to return. Let's save the Jews and start the party."

Really? Do you want to stand before God and explain what happened to the other seventy per cent of humanity? Remember how that worked out for the ones who didn't feed the poor or visit the sick? (Matthew 25)

If God planned that "salvation has come to the Gentiles to make Israel envious," (Romans 11:11) and if "Israel has experienced a hardening in part until the full number of the Gentiles has come in, and in this way all Israel will be saved" (Romans 11:25-26). And if there are almost five billion unbelievers in the world today, how dare we proclaim Judgment Day is right on top of us?

We'd better hope not. Do we think God's love is so weak, or his reach so short, that he doesn't want to bring these people into the fold? And if they're not being reached, who do you think is to blame? God?

No, God has a plan. We call it the Great Commission.

> "Therefore go and make disciples of all nations, baptizing them in the name of the Father and of the Son and of the Holy Spirit, and teaching them to obey everything I have commanded you. And surely I am with you always, to the very end of the age." (Matthew 28:19-20)

All nations, he said. Who are these unreached peoples? The bushmen of southern Africa? The New Tribes of South America? The Dutch of post-Christian Amsterdam? The gangsters of the south side? The pagans of the suburbs—your neighbors, perhaps? Or maybe even the Buddhists, Hindus and Moslems?

Wait, you say, now you've gone too far. Surely not the Moslems. Aren't they outside the mercy of God? The Bible says so, doesn't it? Certainly God hates Esau and presumably his descendants? Well, yes and no. Esau is a whole other subject. Let's look deeper at who the Moslems are and what the Bible says about them.

Start with Ishmael. Remember Ishmael? The father of the Arabs and, through his second son Kedar, the far-removed grandfather of Mohammad.

> Now Sarai, Abram's wife had borne him no children, and she had an Egyptian maid whose name was Hagar. So Sarai said to Abram, "Now behold, the Lord has prevented me from bearing children. Please go in to my maid; perhaps I will obtain children through her." (Genesis 16:1-2)

Sarai is eighty and has no son. First, she blames God, then she suggests giving God a little help? (Have you ever done that?) Why not use her Egyptian slave, Hagar, as a kind of surrogate mother?

You know how that turns out.

> So after Abram had been living in Canaan ten years, Sarai his wife took her Egyptian slave Hagar and gave her to her husband to be his wife. He slept with Hagar, and she conceived. When she knew she was pregnant, she began to despise her mistress. (Genesis 16:3-4)

And Sarai, who concocted this scheme in the first place, whines to Abram, who doesn't want to hear it. "'Your slave is in your hands,' Abram said. 'Do with her whatever you think best.' Then Sarai mistreated Hagar; so she fled from her" (Genesis 16:6). "The Angel of the Lord found Hagar near a spring in the desert .... And he said, "Hagar, slave of Sarai, where have you come from, and where are you going? " (Genesis 16:8).

Don't you love God's rhetorical questions? "Adam, where are you?" It's not that he doesn't know; he wants us to know.

Then the angel tells Hagar two things: First, "I will increase your descendants so much that they will be too numerous to count" (Genesis 16:10). Then he says, "You are now pregnant and you will give birth to a son. You shall name him Ishmael [which means, 'God hears'], for the Lord has heard of your misery" (Genesis 16:11).

Why would God foretell all that for someone outside his plans?

So, Ishmael is born and, when he's about thirteen, God appears to Abram (Genesis 17), makes his great covenant with him, changes his name to Abraham and promises him a son who will inherit the blessing. How does Abraham respond? "If only Ishmael might live under your blessing!" (Genesis 17:18). And God answers:

> As for Ishmael, I have heard you: I will surely bless him; I will make him fruitful and will greatly increase his numbers. He

> will be the father of twelve rulers, and I
> will make him into a great nation. But
> my covenant I will establish with Isaac.
> (Genesis 20-21)

Ishmael is to be blessed?

Years pass and, unfortunately, Ishmael is a normal fifteen-year-old. He mocks little Isaac. Sarah hears him and whines to Abraham. So then, with God's permission, Abraham sends Hagar and Ishmael away with only a bit of food and a skin of water.

> When the water in the skin was gone, [Hagar] put the boy under one of the bushes. Then she went off and sat down about a bowshot away, for she thought, "I cannot watch the boy die." And as she sat there, she began to sob.

> God heard the boy crying, and the angel of God called to Hagar from heaven and said to her, "What's the matter, Hagar? Do not be afraid; God has heard the boy crying as he lies there. Lift the boy up and take him by the hand, for I will make him into a great nation."

> Then God opened her eyes and she saw a well of water. So she went and filled the skin with water and gave the boy a drink.

God was with the boy as he grew up. He lived in the desert and became an archer. While he was living in the Desert of Paran, his mother got a wife for him from Egypt." (Genesis 21:15-20, emphasis added)

Can you imagine growing up as heir in the home—well, tent of a really rich man, then one day finding yourself thrown out? Disowned? Talk about rejection issues. Then what happens? "God heard the boy crying." What does Ishmael's name mean? "God hears." God supernaturally saves Ishmael, then blesses him. The Bible says God was with Ishmael.

What's up with this? Isn't Ishmael supposed to be a bad guy? Aren't the Arabs God's enemies? Are they?

In the entire Bible only four people are named by a divine appearance (an angel or God himself) before they were born. Four. John and Jesus in the New Testament. And, in the Old, Isaac and Ishmael.

Back in the fifteenth chapter of Genesis, God appeared to Abraham in another dream. In that dream he told Abraham how his descendents would move to "a land not their own" and be enslaved for 400 years.

A couple generations pass, and Jacob's sons are plotting to kill their brother Joseph because he lords it over them. And what happens? "They looked up and saw a caravan of Ishmaelites [going] … down to Egypt. Judah said to his brothers, 'What will we gain if we kill our brother and cover up his blood? Come, let's sell him to the Ishmaelites and not lay our hands on him; after all, he is our brother, our own flesh and blood'" (Genesis 37:25-27). So they did.

Do you think it was random chance or divine planning which brought those Ishmaelites by at that moment and both saved Joseph's life and started the dominoes dropping for the prophesied move to Egypt? Israel is in trouble, and God sends Ishmael.

Fast forward a thousand years. Paul writes:

> Just as you who were at one time disobedient to God have now received mercy as a result of [the Jews'] disobedience, so they too have now become disobedient in order that they too may now receive mercy as a result of God's mercy to you. (Romans 11:30-31)

It all ties together.

Consider what Faisal Malick writes in *The Destiny of Islam in the End Times*:

> When God hears the cry of the church on behalf of the Moslems, we're going to see Him do a mighty work. When God hears the cry of Ishmael (the Moslems), he's going to bring them into the kingdom. And when [the Jews] see hordes of Moslems flocking to Jesus they are going to shocked, offended, and the scales will fall from their eyes. And, when God hears the cry of Israel, Jesus Christ is going to return.

Remember, "Blessed is he who comes in the name of the Lord?"

Wait, you ask, why should I care about a bunch of infidel fanatics who are trying to blow up my country and kill me? These are my enemies. Or the illegal immigrants. Or the White, Black, Asian or Hispanic. Or this man or that woman.

No. Moslems are not your enemy. None of those people are your enemy.

Satan is your enemy. (Not even the world or your flesh. Those are the means by which Satan attacks you.) Those other people are under attack, just as you are.

Gerri Dickens said, "You can't experience joy until you love your enemy." Are you experiencing joy?

But, you say, they *are* my enemy.

No, they are your neighbor. Yes, some of them are still slaves to sin and the sin nature, but so are some of you. And white, black, yellow, red or brown, God loves him or her just as much as he loves you. They're your neighbor. What part of loving your neighbor as yourself do you not understand?

Ten separate times the command to "love your neighbor as yourself" from Leviticus 19:18 is repeated in the New Testament. Six of those times are on the lips of Jesus. Do you imagine he considers this important?

But, you say, they don't deserve my love. Isn't that the whole point? Even if they don't deserve or desire God's love and blessing, he loves them anyway—just as he loves us.

God doesn't love you based on your merit or even your need. God loves you because he is God. And you should love these others because they're your neighbor. Jesus' parable of the Good Samaritan illustrates who our neighbor is. (Luke 10: 30-36)

It's the one in need, and the one who sees that need and fills it.

The hero of that parable didn't just help a stranger, he helped someone who probably hated him. First century Jews would travel extra days traveling from Galilee to Judea just to avoid walking through Samaria. Remember the Samaritan woman at the well (John 4:4-26)? She couldn't believe a Jew would condescend to drink water she had drawn. Jesus loves them and commands us to love them likewise.

Okay, you say, what's that have to do with me? I don't know any Moslems. Don't be so sure. Not all Moslems wear *burka*s or *gutra*s.

Even if you don't know any Moslems, you can pray for them. Sincerely, fervently pray. You can support ministries and missionaries who take the Word to them, like Voice of the Truth and Voice of the Martyrs; or who just show them love, like Morningstar Development, Samaritan's Purse or Iris Ministries.

You can't get worked up over saving a bunch of people you've never met? Are you doing any better loving those who live or study or work near you? Jesus said, "Whoever claims to love God yet hates a brother or sister is a liar. For whoever does not love their brother and sister, whom they have seen, cannot love God, whom they have not seen" (1 John 4:20).

Why is Paul willing to give so much to save the Jews? Because he loves them. And so does God. Paul writes, "As far as the gospel is concerned, they are enemies for your sake; but as far as election is concerned, they are loved on account of the patriarchs, for God's gifts and his call are irrevocable" (Romans 11:28-29). Are you doing as much? And isn't that the standard of the kingdom, that we love our neighbor as yourself?

We're so happy that some stone age tribe in the Amazon has been reached or when one of the fourteen million Jews converts, that we forget about the five billion people who aren't Christian. In round numbers, there are over a billion Moslems, a billion Hindus and half a billion Buddhists in the world. The remaining two plus billion are split between the tiny religions and the unaffiliated, including atheists and agnostics. And what about all those folks who think they're Christians but have no clue what that means. The cultural Christians. Jesus loves them. They're your neighbors, too.

Are you prepared to stand before God and tell him that you were so busy preparing for his "welcome back" party that they slipped your mind? Or do you think that Jesus didn't mean to include Moslems, Buddhists, and Hindus in the Great Commission?

I didn't think so.

Pastor Gary asks, are you known for your spiritual gift or for your love? Most Christians don't get beyond the fact that they are saved or they can speak in tongues, but Paul proclaims, "If anyone is in Christ, the new creation has come: The old has gone, the new is here!" (2 Corinthians 5:17). As a new person in Christ, you are his ambassadors to the unsaved. Are you serving the lost?

We forget that we aren't here to be served—by God or man—but to serve. Jesus says, "For even the Son of Man did not come to be served, but to serve, and to give his life as a ransom for many" (Mark 10:45). How many feet have you washed today? We should be humbled that "God has shut up all in disobedience so that He may show mercy to all" (Romans 11:32 NASB).

If we're going to save the Moslems, Buddhists and Hindus, bring the nominal Christians closer to Christ, and excite the Jews to jealousy, and therefore to salvation, we must get our focus off ourselves and onto the Great Commission.

Make no mistake, Jesus is coming again. If we believe everything else we've studied in Paul's letter to the Romans, we need to get busy.

Time may be running out. And if it's soon, we're not ready. Even if it's not, *your* time is limited.

Paul's apparent digression into a personal matter is thus revealed to be part of the great plan—the Great Commission.

Opening his letter to the Romans, Paul outlined how God anticipated and met the need of all fallen humans, shedding his blood, dying and rising from the dead, then pouring out his Spirit to fill and dwell in us. Paul closes his epistle with practical applications of how we are to draw the unsaved toward redemption by our actions. In between (just as he interrupted his discussion of spiritual gifts in his first epistle to the Corinthians with his great ode to love) Paul breaks his discussion of our salvation to emphasize that all of this is dust if it is not done from love. Sacrificial love.

If we don't love our neighbor as our self, if we don't love our worldly enemy as our self, if we don't love the world as Jesus did, then this is all just so much theology.

We will not win the world to Jesus by our words, our thoughts, nor by our signs and wonders. In fact, we shouldn't be praying for signs and wonders: we should be praying for the salvation and healing of others. We will only win others to Jesus by loving them—really loving them—as God so loved the world.

Once we're clear on how we're supposed to relate to our neighbor, only then are we ready to address—as Paul does in the remaining chapters of Romans—how to show love to them in our daily walk.

So Paul closes Romans 11 with this great doxology (33-36):

> Oh, the depth of the riches of the wisdom
> and knowledge of God!
>
> How unsearchable his judgments, and his
> paths beyond tracing out!

"Who has known the mind of the Lord? Or who has been his counselor?" (Isaiah 40:13)

"Who has ever given to God, that God should repay them?" (Job 41:11)

For from him and through him and for him are all things.

To him be the glory forever! Amen.

Study Questions

Chapter 12
God's Plan

1. If God didn't spare the people of the covenant because of their unbelief, why should he spare us?

2. Is it possible that God covered the hearts of the Jews so they didn't understand and accept Jesus precisely to save you? Or your neighbors? Or all the unsaved of the world?

3. Do you expect God to return momentarily? Do you think he's given up on the five billion unsaved? Who do you think God expects to reach those unreached peoples? What should we be doing?

4. Do you love your enemy? Do you love your neighbor? How do they differ?

5. Are you known for your spiritual gifts or your love? Have many feet have you washed?

6. How does a believer in Christ develop such a compassion for those who are lost?

CHAPTER 13

ONE BODY

Romans 12

◆

PAUL RETURNS TO his core argument. We can summarize his good news this way: Our sins are forgiven (Romans 5), we are dead with Christ (Romans 6), but we are in our flesh completely helpless (Romans 7), therefore we rely on the outpoured and indwelling Spirit (Romans 8), as a consequence of which, "We ... are one body in Christ" (Romans 12:5 NASB). Got it?

Just how is this accomplished? Through consecrating ourselves, individually and corporately. By walking in the Spirit. "Therefore I urge you, brethren, by the mercies of God, to present your bodies a living and holy sacrifice, acceptable to God, which is your spiritual service of worship" (Romans 12:1 NASB). Are you willing to give up everything, including what you think God promised? As Abraham was willing to sacrifice his son Isaac?

Remember "presenting"? The brethren here are linked to those in Romans 8:29, "predestined to be conformed to the image of his Son." We are called to present our bodies as a "living and holy sacrifice" to God. Then, and only then, "And do not be conformed to this world, but be transformed by the renewing of your mind" (Romans 12:2a NASB).

Don't skip by this, it's a big deal. As we are, we can't help but relate to the world in a worldly manner; that's how we're built, but, as we present ourselves to God, we are transformed. We are given a new mind to go with our new heart. Like most everything else Paul discusses, this is done by God, not by ourselves.

The presenting is personal, but the sacrifice is corporate: one sacrifice. We present our individual personalities; we become the Body of Christ. "So that you may prove what the will of God is, that which is good and acceptable and perfect" (Romans 12:2b NASB). We then realize our part in God's eternal purpose. Paul addresses this "to every one of you" (Romans 12:3). That "we, who are many, are one body in Christ, and individually members one of another" (Romans 12:5 NASB).

Romans 12:4 draws Paul's famous analogy of our interdependence to the members of a body. "Just as each of us has one body with many members, and these members do not all have the same function." We are not individually the body of Christ; we are members of the body. We cannot survive without one another. I need the help of the body, just as I need the help of the Lord. Why else did Jesus teach us to prayer, "Our Father" rather than "My Father"?

The body isn't an illustration or a metaphor. Like the rest of our salvation, it's a fact. The Bible does not say that the church is like a body, it says that it is the body of Christ. A dozen New Testament citations attest to it.

In Adam I have the life of Adam; essentially individualistic. Only self-interest and distrust; no union, no fellowship. Even after I'm saved, I may be over the problems of sin and the flesh, but I'm still a confirmed individualist. God doesn't blame me for being an individual; but for my individualism. The church's biggest problem is not the outward divisions which split the church—bad as those are—but each of our own individualistic hearts.

Here again the Cross is at work. I died to the independence of Adam and was resurrected a member of his Body, not just as an individual believer.

I don't just seek fellowship; I require connection. If I'm not connected, I die. Just as a burning ember separated from the fire dies, I will die disconnected from the body.

It's no longer myself and my ambitions which should steer me, but whether the body lives and grows. What we need at this point is to see the body of Christ and ourselves as part of it. Only the Holy Spirit can give us that vision. This is how we walk in the Spirit. Remember, we know, we reckon, we present? Now we walk.

Our history started at the fall, but God's plan predated the fall. And it, not the fall, is the template for the ages to come. Genesis 2 sets forth his vision for the church. And sin is not part of the picture. The body of Christ in glory will not reflect fallen man, but be the image of the glorified son of man. "Present unto himself a glorious church" (Ephesians 5:27). Having no spot (scars of sin), or wrinkle (marking age and time lost) nor blemish (imperfection)—giving Satan no grounds to accuse her.

So, here we are. The last times. Satan's power is greater than ever. Our warfare is with "angels, principalities and spiritual powers" (Ephesians 6:12) who attempt to destroy God's work by accusing God's elect. Sin, self-reliance and individualism were Satan's masterstrokes. He fooled us into doing his work for him. But if we put our faith in "Jesus Christ who died" (Romans 8:34), then we are "more than conquerors through him who loved us" (Romans 8:37).

How does this work? Just as we were saved by death and redemption, so death and resurrection are the basis for our life and service. No one can truly serve God without embodying the principles of death and redemption. Even the Lord Jesus served on that basis. He may not have needed to, but in obedience he did. In Matthew 3, Jesus submitted to baptism before he began his ministry. Baptism then and now is a figure for death and resurrection. After he was baptized—voluntarily died and raised from the dead—the Holy Spirit descended upon him. Then he ministered.

Jesus was a sinless man. Yet as a man, he had a separate personality from God.

> Who, although He existed in the form of God, did not regard equality with God a thing to be grasped, but emptied Himself, taking the form of a bond-servant, *and* being made in the likeness of men. Being found in appearance as a man, He humbled Himself by becoming obedient to the point of death, even death on a cross. (Philippians 2:6-8 NASB)

He said, "I do not seek My own will, but the will of Him who sent Me" (John 5:30).

He had a will, but he didn't exercise it. He could have acted from the soul; he didn't. That's what the temptations immediately following his baptism demonstrate. "If you are the Son of God," Satan challenged, prove it. (Matthew and Luke 4) He was trying to trick Jesus into acting for himself—that is, from his soul. Jesus, of course, wasn't fooled. Where Adam acted for himself away from God, Jesus repudiated Satan. As he stated in John 5:19, "the Son can do nothing of Himself." And neither can we. And when we try, we complain that God has failed us!

So, all the work Jesus did on earth was done under the principle of death and redemption. Jesus made this clear to his disciples when, after he had died and been raised, he told them to wait in Jerusalem for "power from on high" to come upon them. What power? The virtue of his death, resurrection and ascension: the presence of the Holy Spirit.

God only recognizes as his ministers those who have come through death to resurrection. In Numbers 17 the Israelites contested Aaron's priesthood. They questioned whether he was really chosen by God. How did God demonstrate it? Twelve dead rods were laid before the Lord in the sanctuary overnight. By morning, only "Aaron's staff, which represented the house of Levi, had not only sprouted but had budded, blossomed and produced almonds" (Numbers 17:8). That dead stick didn't just live, it bore fruit.

Or, look at Romans 7, which deals with a living, personal holiness—trying to please God by our own carnal efforts. The Cross brings Paul—and all of us, if we're honest—to the point where he says, "I can't do it. I can only trust the Holy Spirit to do it in me." So, here we are in Romans 12, and one sphere remains which the death of the Lord must enter before we can truly serve him. Without it, we may be used, but we will often destroy our own work.

It's the matter of our bearing our cross—our daily Christian walk.

In both Galatians and Romans Paul refers to the crucifying aspect of the cross as something already accomplished. "Our old man has been [finally and forever] crucified" (Romans 6:6).

But now we refer to something else, this business of bearing the cross daily. The cross has borne me; now I must bear the cross. Inwardly, continuously. In crucifying our souls, we shift from death to resurrection. We don't lose our souls. It still has all its natural endowments, but now it is subordinated to the Spirit—to God. Paul desired "that I may know Him and the power of His resurrection and the fellowship of His sufferings, being conformed to His death" (Philippians 3:10).

Paul, distrusting all his natural endowments, wrote,

> "For I resolved to know nothing while I was with you except Jesus Christ and him crucified. I came to you in weakness and fear, and with much trembling. My message and my preaching were not with wise and persuasive words, but with a demonstration of the Spirit's power, so that your faith might not rest on men's wisdom, but on God's power." (1 Corinthians 2:2-5)

Look at one passage from each gospel to illustrate bearing our cross—all before Jesus was crucified—starting with Matthew 10:34-39. The soul is the seat of our affections. How much of our lives are influenced by who we love or don't? And so, the Lord declares:

> "Anyone who loves his father or mother more than me is not worthy of me; anyone who loves his son or daughter more than me is not worthy of me; and anyone who

does not take his cross and follow me is not
worthy of me." (Matthew 10:37-38)

To follow the Lord in the way of the Cross is the new
normal; his only way for us. What follows? "Whoever
finds his life will lose it, and whoever loses his life for my
sake will find it" (Matthew 10:39). Our affections can
turn us away from the way of the Cross. And if we do,
we "lose" our soul.

Or Mark 88:34-35. Our Lord told his disciples that
he will suffer and die, Peter protested it, and our Lord
rebuked him as he would Satan. And then Jesus turned
to the crowd and said, "If anyone would come after me,
he must deny himself and take up his cross and follow me.
For whoever wants to save his life will lose it, but whoever
loses his life for me and for the gospel will save it." Again
we have a soul question. The soul desires self-preservation.
And yet we must kill the soul and let God resurrect it.

Am I afraid to do the will of God? You bet! Often
I don't even like the will of God. At precisely that point
God demands that we give in and follow him. Sometimes
the things we have to give up aren't bad things. We may
even think they are good things, but they may not be his
will at that moment.

Our Lord dealt with souls again in Luke 17:32-34.
He's talking about the day the son of man is revealed.
Twice he says, "One will be taken and the other left." He
draws a parallel to Lot fleeing the destruction of Sodom.
Jesus bids us to remember Lot's wife. He tells us on that

day—the last day—one on the housetop and another in the field, and both are warned not to turn back. Why? Because, "Whoever tries to keep his life will lose it, and whoever loses his life will preserve it" (Luke 17:33).

What's he talking about? He seems to be talking about our reaction to the rapture. But wait, doesn't 1 Corinthians 15:51 say, "We will all be changed—in a flash, in the twinkling of an eye, at the last trumpet"? Then why does Jesus discuss our reaction to the call to go? And urgently caution us to be ready?

Perhaps he's warning us that in that instant we will discover our heart's real treasure? Oh, we say we're eager to go. But at that moment when history ends, a backward glance may reveal everything. What if we are more attached to the gifts of God than to the Giver? Or to the work of God rather than God himself? If I'm at my easel, will I try to dab on one more stroke? Will you look back and wish you'd vacuumed the carpet? Or wore higher heels? Grabbed that heirloom? Texted your friends good-bye?

Don't lose sleep over this, worrying about how you'll react, because how you'll react *then* will be determined by whether you live by the soul or by the spirit every day *until then*. If you're tied to the things of this earth, they'll pin you down. The solution is to lose your soul to the Spirit.

Our reaction should be like Peter after the resurrection. He has the guys out in his bass boat and has just made a great haul. And they see someone on the shore. John cries out, "It's the Lord." And what does Peter do? He "threw himself into the sea" (John 21:7). To go to Jesus. Just like that. Splash.

Where is your heart? The Cross must work a detachment in us from everything and everyone outside of the Lord himself.

Look at John 12:24-25 again. "I tell you the truth, unless a kernel of wheat falls to the ground and dies, it remains only a single seed. But if it dies, it produces many seeds. The man who loves his life will lose it, while the man who hates his life in this world will keep it for eternal life."

The inward working of the Cross is fruitfulness. A seed has life in it, but "it remains only a single seed" (John 12:24). It has the power to impart life to others, but to do so it must die. As Jesus did. He passed into death, and his life emerged in many lives. The Son died and came forth as the first of "many sons." He let go of his life that we might receive it.

We're called to die the same way.

Paul wrote, "For we who are alive are always being given over to death for Jesus' sake, so that his life may be revealed in our mortal body. So then, death is at work in us, but life is at work in you" (2 Corinthians 4:11-12).

We who have Christ have new life. Why is there so little expression of it? Why are we "abiding alone?" Why is there no overflowing and imparting of life to others? Because the soul in us envelopes and confines that life, as the husk envelops the grain. We are living in our souls; we are working and serving in our natural strength; we are not drawing from God. We are not living or walking in the Spirit.

Remember Aaron's staff? It endured a night of death, then in the morning it budded. So should we. How do we get resurrection power? By bearing our cross daily—dying to self and living in Christ.

The soul will continue with us until we die. In a very real way, our soul is us—our natural personality, mental and emotional resources. Until our bodies die, we need the day-to-day working of the Cross operating in us. Jesus said, "If anyone would come after me, he must deny himself and take up his cross and follow me" (Mark 8:34). We never get past that. He who evades "is not worthy of me" (Matthew 10:38). He "cannot be my disciple" (Luke 14:27).

"Bearing the cross means likeness to Christ in the principles which animated Him in His path of obedience," Andrew Murray wrote. Watchman Nee said, "Death and resurrection must remain the abiding principle of our lives for the losing of the soul and the uprising of the Spirit of life."

As with our entry into Jesus' death and resurrection for our justification and our sanctification, there must be a crisis that transforms our life and service for God. Like Paul on the road to Damascus. Like Peter quizzed about his love by his Lord by the Sea of Galilee. God must bring us to the point—what John of the Cross called "the dark night of the soul"—where our trust in our natural power is touched and fundamentally weakened—yes, overthrown, so that we no longer dare trust ourselves. Until we no longer like to do Christian work—indeed we almost dread doing things in the Lord's name lest we dishonor him.

We can't follow him out of casual affection: because it makes us feel good. That kind of happiness lasts only a season. Lasting joy comes from making him the focal point of our very existence. Only then, he can begin to use us.

Many of us serve the Lord for the satisfaction we get from doing something for God. But perhaps we aren't doing what God wants us to do. Living by your natural life, you are a slave to your temperament. You run hot and cold. You are not pliable in God's hands. He has to weaken you—break you perhaps—until you will do something because he wants it, not because you like it. Even if it's the same thing. Now you'll do it because it's God's will. Now true joy comes from knowing you're doing his will: a joy deeper than your fluctuating emotions. A joy beyond the happiness of the moment.

God is bringing you to a place where he has but to express a wish and you will respond instantly. No, that doesn't come naturally. It's against everything we know and desire. Initially you will resist it. But until you get there, you should fear yourself. Fear that the impulse you feel came from yourself, not from God.

Once this change happens, you will come to a new place: resurrection ground.

Death may have been wrought by a crisis in your life, but when it has God releases you into resurrection. What you have lost is given back, but not quite as it was before. Self, family, relationships; but all different.

If we want to be spiritual people, we may not need to literally cut off our hands or put out our eyes (Matthew 18:9). Likewise, we can have—must have—a soul. But your soul can't be in charge. As Watchman Nee explains in *Release of the Spirit*, our inner man (our spirit) must break free of its slavery to our outer man (our soul). When the body rules, we live like animals. When the soul rules, we live as rebels and fugitives from God—educated, gifted, cultured; maybe even "good" people—but alienated from God. Only when we live our lives in the Spirit and by the Spirit can God really use us. Yes, even use our bodies and souls, as servants of our spirit and his Spirit.

The difficulty for many of us is that dark night of the soul. At that time we will feel, Gerri Dickens says, as if only we are going through turmoil. Only we are abandoned by God, while all those around us seem blessed and at peace. But that's how it's got to be. You must feel as if he's forsaken you. (You'll be in good company.) And then, at the depths of your fears and sorrows, you'll be tempted to take it all back—to help God.

Don't do it. Keep your hands off the steering wheel. He knows what he's doing. You don't. And if you *still* think you can do a better job, that's proof that your soul is still trying to maintain control.

Gerri says further, there will be a time—it may feel like a long time—when nothing seems to be happening. Everything you value is slipping from you. As if you're locked in a room with no door. It must be so for a night, but that is all. Once your will is broken, you will yield to the slightest touch from God. Nee said, "It is a blessed thing when you know the Lord has met you and touched you in that fundamental way, and that disabling touch has been received."

"Christ's aim is to have me abiding in him," Andrew Murray writes. "All that you have already received—pardon and peace, the Spirit and his grace—are but preliminary to this. All that you see promised to you in the future—holiness and fruitfulness and glory everlasting—are but its natural outcome."

That's it. God knows what he's doing. Then, like Paul, you can claim to serve God "whom I serve in my spirit in preaching the gospel of his Son" (Romans 1:9). You'll have learned the secret of ministry. You'll have joined "we who worship by the Spirit of God, who glory in Christ Jesus, and who put no confidence in the flesh" (Philippians 3:3).

Few can claim to have served God more faithfully than Paul, yet he admitted, "I will not venture to speak of anything except what Christ has accomplished through me in leading the Gentiles to obey God by what I have said and done" (Romans 15:18).

May God make each of us such a "bondservant of Jesus Christ" (Romans 1:1).

Study Questions

Chapter 13
One Body

1. What does it mean to present yourself to God as a living and holy sacrifice? How do you accomplish that?

2. Are you a member of Christ's connected body? Or are you an individual, living life as you think best?

3. How have you followed Jesus through death to resurrection?

4. Do you take up your cross daily? And follow him? How?

5. Where is your heart's treasure? Are you trying to save your life or lose it?

6. What fruit do you bear? Is it to please yourself or in obedience to God?

7. Why do we sometimes emphasize doing church activities and overlook relationships (getting to know people, being open and honest, etc.)? How can you keep these two areas in balance?

8. Why is revenge so devastating to Christians? What does it require of your relationship with God not to take matters into your own hands?

CHAPTER 14

SATISFYING THE LORD

Mark 14: 3-9

BEARING THE CROSS is key to dying to ourselves. Mark's gospel illustrates what Paul says to us in Romans. Jesus has just warned the people not to be found sleeping when the owner of the house returns. The chief priests are seeking a way to arrest and kill Jesus without starting a riot.

> While He was in Bethany at the home of Simon the leper, and reclining at the table, there came a woman with an alabaster vial of very costly perfume of pure nard; and she broke the vial and poured it over His head. But some were indignantly remarking to one another, "Why has this perfume been wasted? For this perfume might have been sold for over three hundred denarii, and the

money given to the poor." And they were scolding her.

But Jesus said, "Let her alone; why do you bother her? She has done a good deed to Me. For you always have the poor with you, and whenever you wish you can do good to them; but you do not always have Me. She has done what she could; she has anointed My body beforehand for the burial. Truly I say to you, wherever the gospel is preached in the whole world, what this woman has done will also be spoken of in memory of her." (Mark 14: 3-9 NASB)

Jesus said wherever the gospel is preached what she did will be spoken of. Well, that's certainly true. But how does he intend for us to understand what she did?

Look at how those present reacted. They grumbled about the waste. To be sure, a year's wages is a lot of money. They were appalled at the waste.

What is waste? Isn't it, among other things, in excess of what's necessary? By it we mean, you give too much and get too little. But Jesus says what she did will be preached to the world. Don't you think he's saying what she did is good?

Look at how the disciples reacted. We know from John's gospel that Judas protested that this money could better have been spent on the poor. (John 12:4-6) We hope we won't be like Peter when we're tested, but it never occurs to us that in our natural state we're just like Judas. He's looking at the bottom line. And he sees total waste. The kind of waste that you've heard people exclaim, "She could have made good if only she weren't a Christian." They see a life wasted. Lived serving Jesus with nothing to show for it.

Pouring out your life for Jesus should flower your soul with glory. Does it? If the Lord be worthy, how can it be a waste? Jesus said, "She has done a good deed to Me." To me. Get it? True good work is not done to the poor or the outcast (that's soulish thinking), true good work is done to Jesus. And nothing is too good for Jesus.

We may not care what Judas thought, but we do care what other Christians think. "When the disciples saw this, they were indignant. 'Why this waste?' they asked. 'This perfume could have been sold at a high price and the money given to the poor'" (Matthew 26:8-9). They thought the same as Judas.

Practical-minded people give or do *just enough* to fulfill whatever purpose is desired. That's not how Jesus thinks. Oh, he wants you and I to be useful, of course, but he clearly has a different measure of merit. What does he want? Jesus wants you to pour out all you have—however much or little it may be—upon him. Whether two mites or a jar of expensive perfume. And if that's all you can do, it's enough.

Because that's our goal: satisfying Jesus.

The Lord isn't interested in all the things we say we do for him. Service to him is not measured by its tangible results. Jesus wants us to pour out all we have—all we are at his feet, as she did. What's in your alabaster jar? What flows out of you once you have died and been resurrected in the Cross? Give it all to Jesus.

The gospel is not just about saving sinners. Sinners will be saved, praise God. But our pleasure in our deliverance is, at best, a by-product of our salvation. No, Jesus died and rose, the gospel was taught, and you were saved so that the Lord may be satisfied. Everything should be to the satisfaction of the Son of God. Only when he is satisfied can we be satisfied. He won't be satisfied until we waste ourselves upon him.

If you don't remember anything else from this study, remember this: in divine service the principle of waste is the principle of power. Our work for him springs out of our ministering to him. It's about him, not his work.

The more it feels as if you're employing your gifts to the limit, the more you find you are living in the principles of this world. We compare ourselves to others—even other Christians—and we judge our closeness to God by what? Our prosperity, our gifts, our recognition, even our looks, the size of our membership list or bank account? No, people. Wrong, wrong, wrong. That's "riding on empty" thinking.

Do you feel that if you followed some other Christian's path—consecrate yourself enough for the blessing, but not for the trouble, enough for God to use you (preferably in front of your friends), but not enough for him to shut you up—that might be sufficient? Would it? Of course, not.

Should you rush out and buy perfume to pour on the altar? No.

"My thoughts are not your thoughts, nor are my ways your ways," Isaiah proclaimed (55:8). To live you must die (Mark 8:35), to gain you must give (Matt 19:21), blessed are those who mourn (5:4), to rule you must serve (Luke 22:26), suffering has a purpose (Romans 5:10-11), and finally no gift is too big.

Take your eyes off others. Look at Jesus. Ask what he values most highly. Here's the principle of waste: "She did it for me, and it was beautiful." True satisfaction comes when we waste ourselves on him. What are we seeking: to be useful? Or to please Jesus?

"It is not what we do for the Lord but what we become to Him that matters," says Francis Frangipane. "It is this inner surrender of the heart, this deliberate turning of our soul Godward, that defines our true progress. Becoming like Jesus is why we exist."

One last point about the woman. Notice that Jesus said, "She poured perfume on my body beforehand to prepare for my burial." Here Jesus introduces another important concept: beforehand.

In the age to come, we'll be called to greater works than anything we've done. "Well done, good and faithful servant! You have been faithful with a few things; I will put you in charge of many things. Come and share your master's happiness!" (Matthew 25:21). Yes, greater work.

But this woman had to do what she did beforehand, because there would be no later opportunity. Watchman Nee wrote:

> I believe that in that [judgment] day we shall all love him as we have never done now, but yet that it will be more blessed for those who have poured out their all upon the Lord today. When we see him face to face, I trust that we shall all break and pour out everything for him. But today—what are we doing today?

Five days after that woman broke the alabaster jar and anointed Jesus' head, some other women went early in the morning intending to anoint the dead body of the Lord. Did they? No. The body was gone—resurrected. Only one soul succeeded in anointing the Lord. This woman, who anointed him beforehand.

Timing is really important.

What are you doing for the Lord today? Is it wasteful? Are you scattering seed like the sower in Christ's parable, or are you carefully planting the seed one at a time?

Our eyes, I hope, have been opened to the preciousness of the one we serve. But have we come to see that nothing but our dearest, our costliest, our more precious is fit for the Lord? Oh, yes, we're doing all sorts of good and useful things, but are we doing them because we think they're good or are we doing them to the Lord? Have we waited on the Lord?

"The idea of waste only comes into our Christianity when we underestimate the worth of our Lord. How precious is he to [you] now?" wrote Watchman Nee.

The Lord said this woman "did what she could." She gave her all. She held nothing in reserve. Don't try to do something for him. That which is external and superficial has no place here. Lay your life at his feet. Today. Beforehand.

Anoint him now, from the depths of your heart, from the very depths of your resurrected being. "Lord, here it is. Take it. It's all yours. Because you are worthy."

"And the house was filled with the fragrance of the perfume" (John 12:3). No one could miss the smell. What does that mean? When you meet someone who has really suffered, immediately your spiritual senses detect the sweet savor of Christ. What is poured out may be lost to the world, but the odor of their action abides.

Make no mistake, this is about who we are, not what we preach or what we do. You cannot produce impressions of God—in yourself or in others—without breaking everything at the feet of the Lord Jesus. Then people will sense Jesus in you. The most unlikely people will detect it. This kind of life creates an impression, that impression creates a hunger, that hunger provokes men to seek him until by divine revelation they discover the fullness of life possible in Christ.

God didn't set us here to preach or do good deeds. He set us here to create a hunger for him in the others of the world. No soul will seek God who doesn't feel a need.

Do you know how restaurants exhaust the smell of their kitchens to make your mouth water as you walk by? You weren't even thinking about food, and suddenly you're ravenously hungry. Hunger has to be created, and can only be created by those who stink with the aroma of God.

Like Elisha. That the Shunemite woman, who had never spoken to him, could say, "I know that this man who often comes our way is a holy man of God" (2 Kings 4:9). The impression left by Elisha was an impression of God.

What impression do you leave? A successful person? A good dresser? A fan of some sin-soaked celebrity, athlete or sports team? Your impact on others turns on one thing: who is the center of your life? If you're a living-in-the-Spirit Christian, it's the working of the Cross to the pleasure of God. Are we willing to break our own hearts in order to satisfy God's heart? We must be willing to release all this for him: our work, our wealth, our children, everything—for God.

It is a blessed thing to be wasted for the Lord. Many of us have been used to the full, but we still don't know what it means to be wasted on God. We think in terms of signs and wonders performed by apostles. God dares us to remember that he put his greatest ambassadors in chains.

God grant us the grace to learn how to please him.

You see, we have an entirely incorrect picture of what God wants for us. We think it has to do with us: our salvation, our sanctification, our eternity in heaven. No, what interests him is what has always interested him, since before he created Adam and Eve. He's interested in our company—our fellowship. To walk and talk with him in the cool of the day, just as Adam and Eve did before they sinned.

God is a god of relationship. He is three in one. He wants to share that with us. But we are unfit, in our present condition, to be in his presence. Therefore, he provided a way to make us fit. He took the initiative and took the burden long before any of us were born. In fact, he started the process before he created heaven and earth.

He invites us to come. He stands at the door and knocks (Revelations 3:20), but we must respond. We must open the door and invite him in. Even more we must surrender ourselves to him.

Frank Bartleman's experience at Azusa Street in Los Angeles left him with the following insight:

> I also received a new revelation of His sovereignty, both in purpose and in action, such as I had never had before. I found that I had often charged God with a seeming lack of interest or tardiness of action, when I should have yielded to Him, in faith, so that He might be able to work through me His sovereign will.

We blame God for indifference because he's not Santa Claus.

We were designed to join him in glory, but first we must join him here. We must bow before him and submit ourselves to his sovereignty and his plan. Gerri Dickens says, "When the Holy Ghost comes you won't have to pray to keep from sinning, and that's only the beginning."

George MacDonald said, "Because we are sons of God, we must become sons of God."

This doesn't mean we don't do acts of love and mercy. We must serve each other and those in need.

We serve Him through them. We serve prayerfully, intentionally, sacrificially.

Study Questions

Chapter 14
Satisfying the Lord

1. Is your life poured out to Jesus? Do people smell your self-righteousness or the aroma of a wasted life? What is your alabaster jar?

2. If there's no power in your life, is it because there's no waste? Can Jesus say of you, "She [or he] did it for me, and it was beautiful?"

3. What are you doing for the Lord today? Is it wasteful? Are you scattering seed liberally or rationing them one by one?

4. Do people hunger after Jesus after "smelling" you?

5. Are you willing to break your heart to satisfy God's? How have you yielded to him?

CHAPTER 15

RELATING TO THE WORLD

Romans 13:1 - 7

◆

HAVING CHALLENGED BELIEVERS for not acting different from the world, Paul explains how the blood, death, resurrection of Christ, and the pouring out and indwelling of the Holy Spirit are normal parts of being a Christian. He examines our responsibility toward non-believers, especially the Jews. Before he closes his epistle, Paul explores how we should live our faith in the midst of a pagan—even hostile world.

Paul opens with a declaration of how we should relate to secular authority. But we must be careful here. We read the words, "Let everyone be subject to the governing authorities, for there is no authority except that which God has established. The authorities that exist have been established by God," (Romans 13:1) through a modern, American filter.

We Americans act as if we, not the Jews, are the chosen people. And that our government is—or is supposed to be—God's agent on Earth. Many of us even think that our particular political faction has some exclusive endorsement of the Lord. Even America's Founding Fathers may have thought so, but not Paul.

The "governing authorities" of his day were people like Pontius Pilate, Herod Agrippa, and the Roman Emperors Caligula and Claudius. You think Nixon, Clinton, Bush, or Obama are bad? Imagine living under megalomaniacs who dipped Christians in tar and set them afire to light their evening parties? Paul instructs us to "be subject to" people like this?

In fact, he advises us,

> Therefore whoever resists authority has opposed the ordinance of God; and they who have opposed will receive condemnation upon themselves. For rulers are not a cause of fear for good behavior, but for evil. Do you want to have no fear of authority? Do what is good and you will have praise from the same. (Romans 13: 2-3 NASB)

Many Americans in 1776 discussed whether they were rebelling against the authority that God had instituted. That verse was a stumbling block for some sincere would-be revolutionaries. Those who decided to rebel anyway did so consciously. They even took pains to excuse themselves in the Declaration of Independence by appealing to "the laws of Nature and of Nature's God." Likewise Christians in Nazi Germany struggled with whether the Bible told them to submit to Adolf Hitler.

But that wasn't Paul's point. Paul tells Christians that Caligula and Claudius and the others were, one, appointed by God and, two, to be submitted to. Why?

> For the one in authority is God's servant for your good. But if you do wrong, be afraid, for rulers do not bear the sword for no reason. They are God's servants, agents of wrath to bring punishment on the wrongdoer. (Romans 13:4-5)

What? Is Paul condoning the murder of believers? Doesn't he understand what was starting to happen to believers all over the Empire? If he doesn't, where is the Holy Spirit? How can such nonsense make it into scripture?

Perhaps it's not nonsense. And perhaps it's relevant today.

Real Christians, as Paul describes them in the previous chapters of Romans, have always been a minority. In fact, they've tended to be persecuted not just by civil authorities but often by the recognized church. Since Roman Emperor Constantine legalized Christianity in AD 313, the church has been armpit deep in politics. Many times the established church and the government worked together to suppress true believers. Perhaps that is what Paul and the Holy Spirit anticipated and addressed.

American Christians have so intermingled religion and politics that we can't distinguish the two. Let me help: we are citizens of the kingdom of God first and foremost; not any nation, any political party, nor even any local church. Many of us believe that our nation, our party, or our congregation are doing the work of the kingdom. I hope so, but not necessarily.

Re-read the whole New Testament. The closest you get to that kind of thinking is right here in Romans 13. Perhaps that's why Paul addresses it. We cannot function as the body of Christ if our allegiance is divided. Your local congregation is at best an extension of the kingdom; not the kingdom itself. Jesus warns us that "no man can serve two masters" (Matthew 6:24).

Really? Then how am I supposed to relate to the government? Paul writes,

> This is also why you pay taxes, for the authorities are God's servants, who give their full time to governing. Give to everyone what you owe them: If you owe taxes, pay taxes; if revenue, then revenue; if respect, then respect; if honor, then honor. (Romans 13: 6-7)

Pay your taxes (all of them), pay revenues (like bridge tolls and entrance fees), be respectful (even if the President or your representative is not of your party), and give appropriate honor. Now it gets tricky. What does Paul mean by "honor"? Obviously, he does not mean that we should prostrate ourselves before images of emperor or party. We dealt with that when we affirmed that "Jesus is Lord" of all.

Jesus instructs, we are to "Render unto Caesar that which is Caesar's" (Matthew 22:21, NASB). And Peter affirms, "Honor the Emperor" (1 Peter 2:17). Honor, but not worship. Honor is the respect due persons of distinction. It doesn't honor the President or governor or mayor to make him the butt of jokes or rumors. Imagine if your national leader is Adolf Hitler, Vladimir Putin or Kim Jong-un. How does a Christian rightly honor such a man?

Paul wrote to Timothy that, "petitions, prayers, intercession and thanksgiving be made for all people— for kings and all those in authority, that we may live peaceful and quiet lives in all godliness and holiness" (1 Timothy 2:1-2). We're to pray blessings on our leaders, not heap ridicule. Because our leaders are, after all, our neighbors, too. Remember loving our neighbor?

These verses reveal the motive for our submission: "that we may live peaceful and quiet lives in all godliness and holiness." Not so we prosper as citizens, not that our party shall prevail, certainly not to advance the agenda of the Hitlers, Stalins or Kims of the world, but so we may pursue godliness and holiness.

So, taxes, revenue, respect, and honor. "Then render to Caesar the things that are Caesar's; and to God the things that are God's" (Matthew 22:21 NASB). And what is God's? What Jesus and Moses tell us, to "Love the Lord your God with all your heart and with all your soul and with all your mind and with all your strength" (Mark 12:30, quoting Deuteronomy 6:5). And what is his second commandment? "Love your neighbor as yourself" (Mark 12:31, Leviticus 19:18).

Remember that Paul wrote to the Christians in Rome before any of the gospels were written, so he didn't know Mark was going to record those words of Jesus. But, whether by his Old Testament scholarship as a Pharisee or by direct revelation from the Holy Spirit, he knew the great commandments.

Study Questions

Chapter 15
Relating to the World

1. Are you subject to the governing authorities? Do you pray for them, even when—especially when—you disagree with their policies? Should you?

2. Do you follow God or a nation, a party, a celebrity or a church? Who is your lord and master?

3. What do you render to Caesar and what to God? Are you sure?

4. What happens to the message of the Gospel and God's reputation when Christians become belligerent and disrespectful in the public sector?

5. What hard decisions do Christians living under oppressive governments have to make? Likewise, what are the pitfalls of living under a benevolent government?

CHAPTER 16

Our Neighbors as Our Burden

Romans 13:8 - 14:12

◆

So, HAVING DEALT with how we relate to the government, Paul turns to our relationship with our neighbors. He writes, "Let no debt remain outstanding, except the continuing debt to love one another, for whoever loves others has fulfilled the law" (Romans 13:8).

This passage affirms how close Paul is to the teachings of Jesus. It could serve as a commentary on Jesus' answer to the rich, young ruler who asked what he must do to be saved. Jesus' answer anticipates what Paul writes here. "The commandments, 'You shall not commit adultery,' 'You shall not murder,' 'You shall not steal,' 'You shall not covet,' and whatever other command there may be, are summed up in this one command: 'Love your neighbor as yourself'" (Romans 13:9).

Paul has just ended his digression on the saving of the Jews, by declaring that God's love extends to all: the saved, the Gentiles (of his day and ours) and the Jews. He expands that message here to prescribe specific behavior by the Christian toward his or her neighbor. "Love does no harm to a neighbor," he says. "Therefore love is the fulfillment of the law" (Romans 13:10).

Jesus didn't just die to save us; he died to consecrate us to God's service. The night before he died, Jesus prayed,

> "Sanctify them by the truth; your word is truth . . . . For them I sanctify myself, that they too may be truly sanctified. My prayer is not for them alone. I pray also for those who will believe in me through their message, that all of them may be one, Father, just as you are in me and I am in you. . . . that they may be one as we are one—I in them and you in me—so that they may be brought to complete unity." (John 17:17-23)

Complete unity. What a heavenly goal: to be one as the Son and the Father are one.

Paul continues, "So let us put aside the deeds of darkness and put on the armor of light" (Romans 13:12). Paul wrote the letter we call Ephesians about three years later than he wrote Romans, but perhaps he was already thinking of the armor of God he described there.

Being armored is being prepared for combat.

Beyond that, he advises us to put on Christ. "Clothe yourselves with the Lord Jesus Christ, and do not think about how to gratify the desires of the flesh" (Romans 13:14). Previously in Romans, Paul describes how to clothe ourselves in Jesus, and many of us trembled at the daunting prospect.

Not gratifying ourselves in our relations with non-believers and new believers may seem even harder. It calls for us to sacrifice our privileges for the sake of others.

"Accept the one whose faith is weak, without quarreling over disputable matters. One person's faith allows them to eat anything, but another, whose faith is weak, eats only vegetables" (Romans 14:1-2). What does eating vegetables have to do with showing love? Quite a bit, as it turns out. Obviously, the issue is not becoming a vegetarian.

In every city of the ancient world, animal sacrifices were made at the local pagan temples. And whatever meat not burned in the offering or eaten by the priests and staff was sold on the local market. So, if you were a Christian, you ate beef or mutton originally dedicated to Jupiter or Artemis.

Think about it, would it give you pause to consider that your meal had been dedicated to some pagan deity? That buying and consuming it supported the worship of some idol? Not today perhaps. We think we're too sophisticated for those superstitions (we have a whole new set), but imagine back then.

Can you understand why it might bother someone who formerly worshiped that pagan god and only recently became a Christian? You—because you know better—are free to eat that meat, but are you showing love to that new believer who struggles over whether to eat only vegetables in order to avoid the risk of eating meat devoted to an idol?

Okay, you say, but meat today doesn't come from pagan temples. Stay with me.

Paul's principle is: "Who are you to judge someone else's servant? To their own master, servants stand or fall. And they will stand, for the Lord is able to make them stand" (Romans 14:4). Praise God. You do not judge your neighbor, but you do bear the burden of his conscience. The day of the week we worship, what we eat and when, or any other practice we perform or avoid is insignificant compared to whether we cause our neighbor to stumble.

Paul writes, "For not one of us lives for himself, and not one dies for himself; for if we live, we live for the Lord, or if we die, we die for the Lord; therefore whether we live or die, we are the Lord's" (Romans 14:7-8 NASB). Do you see where Paul is going?

"But you, why do you judge your brother? Or you again, why do you regard your brother with contempt? For we will all stand before the judgment seat of God" (Romans 14:10 NASB). Don't bear the guilt of leading your neighbor astray. By sneering at his weakness, we don't show love.

"Therefore let us stop passing judgment on one another. Instead, make up your mind not to put any stumbling block or obstacle in the way of a brother or sister" (Romans 14:13). Don't let the exercise of your freedom cause your brother to stumble. Paul continues, "I know and am convinced in the Lord Jesus that nothing is unclean in itself" (Romans 14:14a NASB).

Remember Peter's vision in Acts 10 of the sheet full of unclean animals let down from heaven?

> Peter went up on the roof to pray. He became hungry and wanted something to eat, and while the meal was being prepared, he fell into a trance. He saw heaven opened and something like a large sheet being let down to earth by its four corners. It contained all kinds of four-footed animals, as well as reptiles and birds. Then a voice told him, "Get up, Peter. Kill and eat."
>
> "Surely not, Lord!" Peter replied. "I have never eaten anything impure or unclean."
>
> The voice spoke to him a second time, "Do not call anything impure that God has made clean."
>
> This happened three times, and immediately the sheet was taken back to heaven. (Acts 10:9-16)

We can eat pork or shrimp if we wish, but not if it leads our brother astray. Paul writes, "but to him who thinks anything to be unclean, to him it is unclean" (Romans 14:14b NASB).

Do you understand? Nothing eaten or worn is inherently wrong, but if a brother's conscience convicts him, he is right in abstaining. And so must we for his sake.

Paul continues, "If your brother or sister is distressed because of what you eat, you are no longer acting in love. Do not by your eating destroy someone for whom Christ died" (Romans 14:15). And if what you eat/wear/say confuses your neighbor, you undermine his faith. If you push him to violate his conscience—yes, even something about which your conscience is clear—you are not acting in love.

Oh, we are free. In Colossians 2:21-22, Paul declares, "'Do not handle! Do not taste! Do not touch!'? These rules . . . are based on merely human commands and teachings." You are free to live, worship and serve God with all your might.

John writes, "Yet a time is coming and has now come when the true worshipers will worship the Father in the Spirit and in truth, for they are the kind of worshipers the Father seeks" (John 4:23).

In 2 Samuel 6:12,13-15, we read,

> So David went to bring up the ark of God from the house of Obed-Edom to the City of David with rejoicing. Wearing a linen

> ephod, David was dancing before the LORD
> with all his might, while he and all Israel
> were bringing up the ark of the LORD with
> shouts and the sound of trumpets.

Don't think for a minute that everyone was okay with their king dancing in his Under Armour. "As the ark of the LORD was entering the City of David, [his wife] Michal daughter of Saul watched from a window. And when she saw King David leaping and dancing before the LORD, she despised him in her heart" (2 Samuel 6:16).

David was so happy that the Ark of God was finally coming to Jerusalem that he stripped off his kingly robe and, wearing nothing but a linen undergarment, danced in front of the procession. He didn't just waltz, "he danced with all his might" leaping and skipping. He worshipped God in spirit and truth.

When you feel like worshipping the Lord with that much abandon, you are free to do so. In fact, of course, you should.

And if your brother or sister dances before the Lord, don't you criticize. His wife Michal despised David for his lack of inhibition. She said, "How the king of Israel has distinguished himself today, going around half-naked in full view of the slave girls of his servants as any vulgar fellow would!" (2 Samuel 6:20).

Can't you just see her sniffing and looking down her nose at his sweat? She was worried about what others thought. David answered, "I will celebrate before the

Lord. I will become even more undignified than this, and I will be humiliated in my own eyes. But by these slave girls you spoke of, I will be held in honor" (2 Samuel 6:21-22).

If you are moved to dance or sing or serve, do so. And if others sing or dance or serve differently from you, don't judge them. When our Lord taught, "Do not judge, or you too will be judged" (Matthew 7:1), during his Sermon on the Mount, he included the explanation, "For in the same way you judge others, you will be judged, and with the measure you use, it will be measured to you" (Matthew 7:2).

Don't be looking for the speck in your brother's eye. And don't let your freedom harden the chains which enslave your brother or sister.

Study Questions

Chapter 16
Our Neighbors as our Burden

1. How do you love your neighbor? Does your neighbor feel loved by you? Can God see any evidence of it?
2. Has your neighbor stumbled because of you? How do you know?
3. Found any specks in your brother's eye recently?
4. How can you clothe yourself with Jesus?

CHAPTER 17

HAVING THE SAME ATTITUDE

Romans 14:17 - 16:27

◆

How DOES OUR being free relate to loving our neighbor?

Paul writes, "All things are lawful for me, but not all things are profitable" (1 Corinthians 6:12). Not only that but, returning to Romans 14, he continues,

> For the kingdom of God is not eating and drinking, but righteousness and peace and joy in the Holy Spirit. For he who in this way serves Christ is acceptable to God and approved by men. So then we pursue the things which make for peace and the building up of one another. (Romans 14:17-19 NASB)

It sounds easy, but this is a hard teaching. Yes, you are free to do as you please, but you are also constrained by love. If the Holy Spirit is in us, we, like Jesus, will pour ourselves out for others. Why? For love. And obedience—doing what the Father commands.

A total openness should exist between you and God in which you can be you and you can dwell in Jesus. "Abide in Me, and I in you" (John 15:4 NASB). Thank the Lord. But between you and your neighbor—especially your unsaved or newly-saved neighbor—you must be wise and loving.

> Blessed is the one who does not condemn himself by what he approves. But whoever has doubts is condemned if they eat, because their eating is not from faith; and everything that does not come from faith is sin. (Romans 14:22-23)

This may seem simple minded to you, but our churches have violated this teaching almost as long as there have been churches. Christians have fought and killed each other over the form of communion elements, over gestures of supposed humility, over matters of personal precedence. How many of you grew up in churches which expected men to wear hats outdoors but not in, and women to have their heads covered all the time, but not wear makeup anytime? Who used grape juice for communion and called those who didn't drunkards? That's obviously not right. No, just as God undoubtedly approved David's uninhibited dance worship, he wants us not—by our behavior or our words—to place stumbling blocks in front of the weak.

Paul writes, "So then we pursue the things which make for peace and the building up of one another" (Romans 14:19 NASB).

Jesus says to his disciples, "Things that cause people to stumble are bound to come, but woe to anyone through whom they come. It would be better for them to be thrown into the sea with a millstone tied around their neck than to cause one of these little ones to stumble" (Luke 17:1-2). In this context, the little ones are those weak in the faith.

We are free to strip off our clothes and dance around naked before God, but we should do it at home … with the curtains drawn. Not because we're afraid of what the neighbors will think of us, but because we don't want to lead our neighbor astray. Our neighbor whom God loves and who may not yet see the difference between worshipping God and enticing to sin.

Wait, you say, what's this got to do with me? Meat isn't sacrificed to idols today. I don't dance around in my BVDs. No, but the idols are all around us: sports figures, politicians, musicians and actors. If we wear the jersey of some red-hot but sin-soaked sports star, what does it say to our neighbor? If we watch the latest gore-fest or orgy at the cinema, then praise it on social media, what do the unsaved think? When we campaign for politicians who are racists or support unnatural marriage or killing babies, what does that say to our neighbor?

Yes, you are free, but you are also a child of the king.

People are watching you. Judging him by your actions.

> For even Christ did not please himself
> but, as it is written: 'The insults of those
> who insult you have fallen on me.' For
> everything that was written in the past was
> written to teach us, so that through the
> endurance taught in the Scriptures and the
> encouragement they provide we might have
> hope." (Romans 15:3-4)

He also writes, "God has chosen to make known among the Gentiles the glorious riches of this mystery, which is Christ in you, the hope of glory" (Colossians 1:27).

If we know that Christ in us is the hope of glory and we are to love our neighbor as ourselves, can we not reckon (remember knowing and reckoning?) how we must act toward our neighbors, even relative to times and technologies unknown to Paul?

> May the God who gives endurance and
> encouragement give you the same attitude
> of mind toward each other that Christ Jesus
> had, so that with one mind and one voice
> you may glorify the God and Father of our
> Lord Jesus Christ. Accept one another,
> then, just as Christ accepted you, in order
> to bring praise to God. (Romans 15:5-7)

One mind and voice, like a choir. Singing in harmony. Praising God as he has gifted each of us. Complementing— not competing with one another. Certainly not leading each other astray.

He urges us to have the same attitude toward each other as Jesus. Paul writes,

> Being like-minded, having the same love, being one in spirit and of one mind. Do nothing out of selfish ambition or vain conceit. Rather, in humility value others above yourselves, not looking to your own interests but each of you to the interests of the others. (Philippians 2:2-3)

Do you hear what he's saying? We weren't saved, we weren't filled with the Holy Spirit, we aren't citizens of the kingdom of God for our pleasure and our benefit. But, in humility and love, for others.

Remember the Great Commission (Matt 28:18-20)? How are we to make disciples of our neighbors and how can we disciple them, if we don't love them? Love them as Christ loved us?

C. S. Lewis called this the weight of glory. "The … burden of our neighbor's glory [is] laid on my back, a load that only humility can carry."

"Next to the Blessed Sacrament itself," he wrote, "your neighbor is the next holiest object presented to your senses." Why is that? Because everything else we experience will eventually pass away. That ham sandwich, that dress, that car, the United States, the world, the sun, the entire universe are all destined for destruction. But the man or woman you so casually pass on the street will, like yourselves, exist for the rest of eternity.

How then, in love, can we do less for our neighbor?

Paul adds these words of encouragement:

> For I tell you that Christ has become a servant of the Jews on behalf of God's truth, so that the promises made to the patriarchs might be confirmed and, moreover, that the Gentiles might glorify God for his mercy. As it is written: "Therefore I will praise you among the Gentiles; I will sing the praises of your name." Again, it says, "Rejoice, you Gentiles, with his people." And again, "Praise the Lord, all you Gentiles; let all the peoples extol him." And again, Isaiah says, "The Root of Jesse will spring up, one who will arise to rule over the nations; in him the Gentiles will hope. (Romans 15:8-12)

Remember who the Gentiles are? The five billion unsaved. The Hindus, Buddhists, Moslems and atheists. Your neighbors and mine, perhaps the next person you talk to.

We aren't isolated disciples of our Lord Jesus. We have been given great gifts: forgiveness of our sins, rebirth in Christ, death of our sin nature, the outpouring and the in-dwelling of the Holy Spirit.

But these treasures aren't given just for our own pleasure. We're one body in Christ, so the great law of love binds us—yes, binds us to act in all love and humility for the common salvation of our brothers and sisters. The normal Christian life Watchman Nee speaks of.

Isaiah wrote,

> "This is what the LORD says—your Redeemer, the Holy One of Israel: 'I am the LORD your God, who teaches you what is best for you, who directs you in the way you should go'" (Isaiah 48:17).

And just what way does he direct us? Jesus, of course. Who declared, "I am the way and the truth and the life. No one comes to the Father except through me." (John 14:6)

Many non-believers reject Christianity out of hand because of that one claim of Jesus. They find it narrow and exclusive. But if they'd listen to all that Jesus said—and look at what he did—they'd realize that God's invitation is broad and inclusive. In the very next verse, Jesus says, "If you really know me, you will know my Father as well. From now on, you do know him and have seen him" (John 14:7).

"From now on?" How's that work? Jesus ascended to Heaven two thousand years ago. How are they to know Jesus in this age? I'll tell you: through the direct action of the Holy Spirit and the indirect action of those within whom the Holy Spirit dwells.

Whether and how we love our neighbors may be the only gospel many of them ever see. Yes, we're free to live our lives with abandon, but we're are also constrained by our love—and not as the world love, but God's love working in us through the Holy Spirit—to show Jesus, the way, to those neighbors whom God brings into our paths. We—the Holy Spirit working in and through us—are the hope of the world.

> The commission God gave me to present to you the word of God in its fullness—the mystery that has been kept hidden for ages and generations, but is now disclosed to the Lord's people. To them God has chosen to make known among the Gentiles the glorious riches of this mystery, which is Christ in you, the hope of glory. (Colossians 1:25-27)

As it was in the first century, so it is in the twenty-first century. Christ in you—his Holy Spirit—is the hope of the world.

Paul then blesses the Christians in Rome (and us), "May the God of hope fill you with all joy and peace as you trust in him, so that you may overflow with hope by the power of the Holy Spirit" (Romans 15:13).

Are you filled with "all joy and peace"? Are you "overflow[ing] with hope"? If not, why not? It's available. Moreover, it's God's plan for you. Jesus suffered and died and rose to bring it about. The Holy Spirit has been poured out on you and could be dwelling within you to that end. If it's not happening in our lives, maybe we are the blockage.

Look at the next verse.

"I myself am convinced, my brothers and sisters, that you yourselves are full of goodness, filled with knowledge and competent to instruct one another" (Romans 15:14). How can Paul write that? Didn't he open this letter castigating the Romans (and us) for not being good or knowledgeable or competent? (Romans 1:18 – 3:20). How can he now be convinced that we're good to go? What has changed? Hopefully, reading and applying his message, we have changed.

Paul spent the intervening five thousand words instructing us that God the Father is the source of our goodness, that God the Son is the word of life, and God the Holy Spirit walks beside us to reveal all we need. "But the Advocate, the Holy Spirit, whom the Father will send in my name, will teach you all things and will remind you of everything I have said to you" (John 14:26).

God is with you now. Receive the Holy Spirit. Take your hands off the steering wheel of your life. Give glory to God. And love your neighbor.

Paul closes Romans with a longer than usual list of greetings and blessings. He may do so to remind his readers that he is a legitimate apostle, not some letter writer whom no one ever heard of.

Regardless, tucked into that list is a significant warning about causing divisions or putting obstacles in the way of other believers. "Such people are not serving our Lord Christ, but their own appetites" (Romans 16:18). Our "appetites" covers a world of mischief. Not only our carnal desires, but also our fleshly pride, knowledge and willfulness. When we serve ourselves, we aren't serving him. And, as long as we serve ourselves, we betray the great commission. How can we win the world for Jesus when we quench the Spirit within us?

Listen: Each of us who are called by Christ have the presence of the living God within us. Now; every day. We have the Bible and preachers and teachers and evangelists and prophets, and we are thankful for them. But preachers and teachers—even the Bible—are not substitute for the voice of God. We can't even understand the Bible unless the Spirit reveals it to us. To the rest of the world this is foolishness.

> But we preach Christ crucified: a stumbling block to Jews and foolishness to Gentiles, but to those whom God has called, both Jews and Greeks, Christ the power of God and the wisdom of God. For the foolishness of God is wiser than human wisdom, and the weakness of God is stronger than human strength. (1 Corinthians 23-25)

Each of us can—and should—have access to the voice of God daily. You don't need anyone else to direct you in the paths of righteousness; let his Spirit lead you. David wrote, "He guides me in the paths of righteousness For

His name's sake" (Psalm 23:3 NASB). He, who? The good shepherd. The spirit of Jesus, with us now and forever. "The person without the Spirit does not accept the things that come from the Spirit of God but considers them foolishness, and cannot understand them because they are discerned only through the Spirit" (1 Corinthians 2:14).

If we're failing to hear him perhaps we're letting the world, the flesh and, yes, the accuser drown out the still, small voice of God. But his voice is available to us nonetheless. As Sharon Ruffin says, "Don't get distracted; listen to God. Stay focused on what God is saying and doing." Let everything that obstructs or gets in the way come down.

Open yourself to God, and listen to Him only. Read the Bible; listen to Christian music; come hear messages of hope and guidance; but first and last pray. Don't bore Him with your list of demands. He already knows your heart.

Listen. Listen to God. He's talking to you. "For God does speak—now one way, now another— though no one perceives it" (Job 33:14).

Crystolin Macklin reminds us,

> You can't focus on what it looks like in someone else's life or what it looked like before. God is doing something new in everyone's life. He'll do it, when, where and how he wants to; then change it all the next time. [God] isn't anything we can manage. No, 'It's gonna be good.' You have to trust him.

"'What no eye has seen, what no ear has heard, and what no human mind has conceived' — the things God has prepared for those who love him—these are the things God has revealed to us by his Spirit" (1 Corinthians 2:9-10). Because God is "able to do immeasurably more than all we ask or imagine, according to his power that is at work within us" (Ephesians 3:20).

Yes, more than we can imagine.

And so Paul closes, (Romans 16:25-27):

> Now to him who is able to establish you in accordance with my gospel, the message I proclaim about Jesus Christ, in keeping with the revelation of the mystery hidden for long ages past, but now revealed and made known through the prophetic writings by the command of the eternal God, so that all the Gentiles might come to the obedience that comes from faith—to the only wise God be glory forever through Jesus Christ! Amen.

Study Questions

Chapter 17
Having the Same Attitude

1. How do you reconcile your freedom and loving your neighbor? How do your thoughts, words and deeds lead to peace and mutual edification?

2. How do you love Christians of other traditions? Even those whose beliefs are contrary to yours?

3. How heavy does the burden of glory feel? Do you feel as if you're bearing it alone?

4. What is the ultimate purpose for Christians getting along with one another?

5. How can your worship of God be enhanced by thinking about what God is like?

6. When was the last time you listened—really listened—to God? What did he say? How did you respond?

CLOSING

WHY HAVE YOU never heard this message before?

Why isn't Paul's letter to the Romans being taught this way today?

It is. Men like Charles Spurgeon and Andrew Murray in the nineteenth century, A. W. Tozer, Watchman Nee and Billy Graham in the twentieth, and Rick Joyner and Francis Frangipane currently share similar messages. But, no, this interpretation isn't in the mainstream of Western biblical thought.

Perhaps it's because modern Christianity is dominated, when it isn't chasing after the world trying to be relevant, by a great debate between the "insurance" Christians and the "fireworks" Christians, over which is the most authentic branch of Christianity, with each cherry picking those portions of scripture to support their side. One group declares that the spiritual gifts ceased after the apostolic generation, yet they pray for the sick. Another group teaches that if you don't speak in tongues you aren't really filled with the Holy Spirit. Still another group busies itself calculating the date of Jesus' return. These debates divert attention from what God offers—what the Bible really reveals to us. Looked at their way, the Bible might as well be so much Greek.

Quit it. Quit looking for support for your prejudices; quit trying to earn your way into heaven; quit seeking the social advantages of being a Christian; quit being satisfied with being saved; quit puffing yourself up because you exhibit this or that gift of the Spirit; quit condemning others for the same thing you do; quit looking for dreams and visions (even of heaven).

Just quit it and look to Jesus. Take up your Cross and start killing yourself. Break the dominance of your soul, so it and your body may be resurrected in unity with the Holy Spirit and we can start—yes, start the serious business of becoming the Bride of Christ. Becoming holy. Because that is the focus of God's plans and Paul, Augustine, Luther, Wesley and Nee's writing: the church.

We as the church, are we unwrinkled, unblemished, spotless? Hardly.

We have a long way to go. Let's start by opening ourselves to the Holy Spirit. Surrendering ourselves to the Holy Spirit. Start living in the Spirit daily. Taking up our cross and following Jesus even unto death, with the assurance that resurrection awaits us beyond the grave. Waits for us now. "Not [living] according to the flesh but according to the Spirit" (Romans 8:4).

Are you humble enough to admit that God's work in you isn't finished? Are you willing to allow him deeper?

Just how badly do you want Jesus? Badly enough to die? Badly enough to be ridiculed? Badly enough to be broken and poured out? "If by the Spirit you put to death the misdeeds of the body, you will live" (Romans 8:13).

Are you ready to waste your life for God? So that we may be a sweet aroma in his nostrils and excite that same hunger in those around us for the same blessings we've received.

We certainly don't need a bunch of folks telling us Jesus is coming back tomorrow. "At that time if anyone says to you, 'Look, here is the Messiah!' or, 'Look, there he is!' do not believe it. For false messiahs and false prophets will appear and perform signs and wonders to deceive, if possible, even the elect" (Mark 13:21-22). Yes, we're in the last days. We have been since Pentecost. None of us knows when our souls will be required of us (Luke 12:20). Time is short and therefore urgent.

Don't chase fads and false prophets. Take God at his word and do as he says.

"Jesus Christ is the same yesterday and today and forever" (Hebrews 13:8). He won't mislead you into the latest apocalyptic fad. American Christians have been speculating about the Second Coming for two hundred years, and all we do is discredit God to the unbelieving world.

What part of the great commission told us to sit around guessing when Jesus will return? In fact, Jesus rather specifically told us we wouldn't know. "Why do you stand here looking into the sky?" (Acts 1:11). Keep watch, yes; speculate, no. (Revelations 3:3, Matthew 24:42, 25:13, Mark, Ecclesiastes 9:12) Why are we disobeying? Quit it.

Rick Joyner exhorts us not just to make converts, but disciples. Don't just be Christians; we weren't saved just to be Christians, but to be disciples.

So, you may ask, if the Holy Spirit is present and if God's purpose is still being revealed, why isn't God writing epistles like Romans today?

He is.

You are the letters God is writing to this world. As Paul writes, "You yourselves are our letter … known and read by everybody. You are a letter from Christ … written not with ink but with the Spirit of the living God, not on tablets of stone but on tablets of human hearts" (2 Corinthians 2 3:2-3).

All some people will see of Jesus is you. What do they see? Does his light so shine in your life that you are a beacon to the lost and lonely? Francis of Assisi advises us to "Preach the gospel always; If necessary use words."

The underlying message of Romans is that God loves us—all of us—and wants us to be with Him forever as his children. "For those who are led by the Spirit of God are the children of God" (Romans 8:14). He made the way. All we must do is respond in faith.

Paul's benediction summarizes his letter and reminds us both of our connection to God's promises and works in the past and also of his promises and work—work we the church are to participate in—in the future. Not surprisingly his closing words parallel Jesus' Great

Commission for us to "Go therefore and make disciples of all the nations" (Matthew 28:19-20).

> Now to him who is able to establish you in accordance with my gospel, the message I proclaim about Jesus Christ, in keeping with the revelation of the mystery hidden for long ages past, but now revealed and made known through the prophetic writings by the command of the eternal God, so that all the Gentiles might come to the obedience that comes from faith—to the only wise God be glory forever through Jesus Christ! Amen. (Romans 16:25-27)

God isn't finished with you. He's hardly begun. Through him all things are possible. Paul's revelations in his letter to the Christians in Rome is just the beginning.

"Anything that God has ever done for a soul He will do for anyone else, if the conditions are met," A. W. Tozer wrote.

What might he do in you if you trust and obey him?

Are you ready to waste your life for God?

Study Questions

Closing

1. What must change to bring you closer to God?
2. Pastor Gary Garner says, "Obedience is not just will power, but the Spirit upon us. Your spiritual weapon is the cross. Bear it." How does that apply to you?
3. "Moses said to [God], "If your Presence does not go with us, do not send us up from here."" (Exodus 33:15) How does God's presence manifest itself in your life? Is that satisfactory? What do you need to change?

ACKNOWLEDGEMENTS

FIRST I ACKNOWLEDGE and humbly apologize to the Holy Spirit for being such a slow learner. I have been a Christian for over fifty years, but I am only now becoming what I should have been all along. Most of these ideas weren't mine, but gleaned from half a century of study, listening and prayer.

I thank my spiritual mentors—Doris Andrea, Mildred Adams, John H. Hodge, José P. Bové, Wallace Gray, Charles Avery, Charles Baldwin, Gary Durham, Ted Haggard and Gary Garner—for leading me to Christian growth at each stage of my life. I especially thank my friends at Prevailing Word Ministries for encouraging me to develop this message, which has changed my life if not theirs. None of them are responsible for the errors I have made in this study, but each deserves credit for preparing me for the next level of Christian growth—like runners passing me forward similar to a baton.

Lastly I wish to acknowledge and thank my wife of these many years, Treva. Without her presence and her eager search for more of the truth of the gospel, I might have remained one of those comfortable nominal Christians sitting in some church's back pew once a week for the rest of my life.

Prevailing Word Ministries

THIS STUDY WAS written at the behest of Prevailing Word Ministries of Glen Allen, Virginia.

Prevailing Word's mission is to establish and maintain a dwelling place in the spirit for the worship of Almighty God, our heavenly Father, within our community, and throughout the world. To preach the gospel of Jesus Christ and make disciples of all nations.

Visit

PWM at 1656 Mountain Road, Glen Allen, VA 23060

or on their website at
http://prevailingwordministriesva.org/

Printed in the United States
By Bookmasters